YOUR
RETIREMENT
INCOME
BLUEPRINT

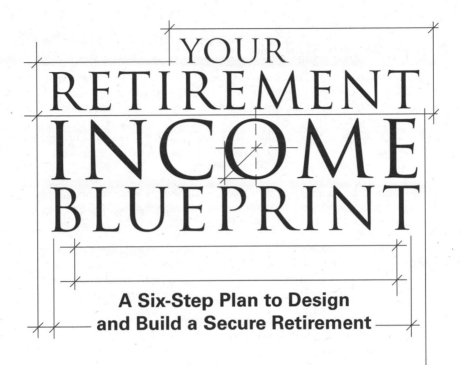

YOUR RETIREMENT INCOME BLUEPRINT

A Six-Step Plan to Design and Build a Secure Retirement

DARYL DIAMOND

A CANADIAN GUIDE

WILEY

John Wiley & Sons Canada, Ltd.

Library and Archives Canada Cataloguing in Publication Data

Diamond, Daryl, 1953–
          Your retirement income blueprint : a six-step plan to design and build a secure retirement / Daryl Diamond.

Includes index.

          1. Retirement income—Canada—Planning. .I. Title.

HG179.D447 2011   332.024'014   C2011-901438-6

978-1-118-08752-7 (print), 978-1-118-08983-5 (ePDF), 978-1-118-08979-8 (eMobi), 978-1-118-08978-1 (ePub)

Production Credits
Interior design and typesetting: Adrian So
Cover design: Adrian So
Printer: Solisco Tri-Graphic Printing Ltd.

John Wiley & Sons Canada, Ltd.
6045 Freemont Blvd.
Mississauga, Ontario
L5R 4J3

Printed in Canada
1 2 3 4 5 STG 15 14 13 12 11

ENVIRONMENTAL BENEFITS STATEMENT
Using 4,250 lbs. of Rolland Enviro100 Print instead of virgin fibres paper reduces John Wiley & Sons Canada, Ltd. ecological footprint by:

TREES	SOLID WASTE	WATER	AIR EMISSIONS
36 FULLY GROWN	**1,041** KILOGRAMS	**98,498** LITRES	**2,287** KILOGRAMS

It's the equivalent of :
Tree(s) : 0.7 american football field(s)
Water : a shower of 4.6 day(s)
Air emissions : emissions of 0.5 car(s) per year

To Karen, Geoff and Kelly
for making it all so amazing

CONTENTS

PREFACE

THE EVOLUTION OF A BOOK
AND OF A DEMOGRAPHIC

In 2002, I had the opportunity to publish a work entitled *Buying Time*. When *Buying Time* was first written, the leading edge of the Baby Boom generation was turning 55. Now, as those on the cusp of that generation turn 65 and begin applying for their Old Age Security, we are in the midst of a "perfect (retirement) storm." The transition from the accumulation years to the income years is now a front-and-centre issue for retiring Baby Boomers (and those hoping to retire soon), and rightly so. They're concerned about our present economic environment and some issues that await us in the future. Common concerns include:

- the wave of Boomers is just starting to turn 65 in 2011
- historically low interest rates
- a stock market disaster in late 2008 and early 2009, which still has many unnerved
- significant upcoming changes to the Canada Pension Plan, particularly affecting those between the ages of 60 and 65
- limited private sector participation in defined benefit pension plans
- government debt, which is already high and will continue to increase as the demand for government-provided medical care is going skyrocket over the next 20 years

As a result of these and other factors, those coming up to retirement (as well as some already in retirement) are desperately looking for solutions. And while I will be making references to the Baby Boom generation, the principles and strategies presented in this book apply to anyone within 10 years of a target retirement date and those who have retired within the past 10 years.

The information contained within this book is the result of over 20 years of putting together retirement income plans for retirees and then working with them, through the years, as their retirement life changes. As an advisor who is one of the pioneers in the retirement income area of financial planning, I have worked through different rates of inflation, changes to the taxation of income and assets, as well as dramatic swings in both the stock market and interest rates. I have lived through them along with my clients, and I have worked through them with my clients. As I like to say, I have retired a few hundred times—vicariously, through the clients I serve. As such, I am able to include in this book the practical application of what we have found to be effective strategies as well as the experience and insights of having worked in this area of financial planning since 1988. My business practice, which is composed of qualified planners and support staff, is dedicated to serving retirees.

There is no question that each retirement scenario is unique and each situation must be weighed on its own merits. The material put forward in this book is predicated on what has been employed successfully with my clients. I am able to share with you nearly a quarter of a century's experience and insight into this process.

It is my goal to bring together various concepts and strategies and, in doing so, to show you how to create more enjoyable retirement years through a comprehensive planning process and the efficient use of your assets.

This is not intended to be a "do it yourself" book. By facilitating more comprehensive communication between investors and advisors, it is intended to be a "do it properly" and "do it better" book.

INTRODUCTION

Golf Clubs or Hockey Sticks?

It is common to use a golf game as an analogy when comparing the years when we are accumulating assets and the years when we are drawing income from those assets. To acknowledge that there is a difference between these two times in one's life, the comparison suggests that those years when we are saving money and building retirement assets are the "front nine." The "back nine" represents the time when we are withdrawing money from personal assets, pensions and government benefits in order to create the cash flow required to fund retirement. Well, in my experience, that comparison is only partially accurate.

Let's maintain the premise that the accumulation years are like playing the front nine in a game of golf. You finish those first nine holes, and then you go into the clubhouse for lunch. When you come out of the clubhouse and start taking income, the analogy needs to change. Imagine that instead of stepping on the tenth tee, you are stepping onto a freshly flooded ice rink. The playing field changes because there are such substantial differences between the planning approaches, investment strategies, risk-management issues and sheer dynamics of these two phases in someone's life. It is not simply a continuation of the same thing.

The point here is that if you are attempting to play the game of hockey using the same equipment and same skill sets that you use to play golf, you are not going to do a very efficient job. But that is how different things become when it is time to draw retirement income. You need to be aware of this and so does the advisor or institution with whom you align yourself.

There are many concepts and well-known rules of thumb for the accumulation years that do not apply in the same way, or apply at all, in the income years. Some of the traditional approaches are, in fact, detrimental to creating the most efficient income stream. Planning retirement *income* is a very different art and science than planning the accumulation of assets, and there are few advisors who are proficient in it. That is what is missing for consumers.

That may be why you picked up this book. You know there is something more to this whole "retirement income process," but you just aren't sure what that is. You feel something is missing in your current situation, but you don't know what, and you don't know where to find it. This has never been more important than it is now, as you seek a greater level of comfort, security and enjoyment in your retirement.

Why You *Need* a Blueprint

How can you have an understanding and a clear view of how this is all going to piece together for you if there is no plan in place and no process for you to work through as you move through the many phases that will make up your retirement years? You can't, unless you have your own blueprint.

A blueprint is formally defined as a technical drawing that represents an architectural or an engineering design. More generally, and in the context I use it here, the term "blueprint" has come to refer to any detailed plan.

The operative word here is detailed. I have seen so-called plans that consist of two or three pages of cursory projections and fifteen pages of product recommendations. That is not detailed planning. That is pushing products, and it is offered far too often to consumers and may explain why there is so much confusion in the marketplace. The retirement income area of financial planning is not a product-driven market. Products do assist in providing solutions but, done properly, the emphasis is first on planning and process.

Your blueprint is a detailed plan that incorporates processes, proven strategies and a defined course of action. It should not only be efficient in terms of asset use and taxation but it should also be custom designed to assist you in achieving those things you wish to do in retirement. Keep in mind that it needs to be put together by someone who is proficient in this area of planning.

Putting It Together by Taking It Apart

When a person retires, he or she goes from one source of income (employment income) to six, seven or more sources of cash flow. When I first meet with people who are looking at retirement, they consistently tell me that they are looking for someone who can take all of these different forms of income and the assets they have and put it all together for them. This book will show you the processes to do this. Ironically, to put it all together, you'll also have to plan how you are going to take things apart.

What I mean by that is this. Financially speaking, retirees fall into three general groups. One group has very few assets and/or benefits and relies heavily on government benefits or transfers for their retirement income. Another group is fairly affluent, and I refer to them affectionately as "coupon clippers." These people have enough personal wealth to derive the majority, if not all, of their retirement income from the interest and dividends that are earned by the money they have invested. They will likely use little, if any, of the actual invested capital.

The third group includes about 70 to 75 per cent of Canadian retirees. They have sufficient assets to permit them to retire, but will need to use varying amounts of their invested capital in order to create the cash flow they require over the duration of their retirement. As such, some "intelligent disassembly" is required. And this is one of the key purposes of the blueprint. A properly structured blueprint can help to effectively address all of these considerations:

- Which income streams should be accessed and in what order?
- Which assets should be used first and which ones deferred for later use?

- How can less tax be paid and government entitlements be preserved?
- How will the combination of all of these actions impact net worth going forward?

The purpose of this book is to provide you with a more specific awareness and understanding of retirement income planning and how it applies to you. At the same time, I want to show you examples of the application of these processes, concepts and strategies to illustrate how they may be of benefit to you. The end goal is to help you make the most efficient use of your money and your time when you retire.

And to do that you need to have a blueprint. A key part of developing your personal blueprint starts with the exercise of establishing your own objectives and priorities. This will allow you, and your partner if applicable, to better understand and emotionally relate to what it is you wish your retirement experience to be. By implementing the processes contained within this book, you will have a more orderly and structured retirement. Things will make sense and seem less chaotic. And in having more structure, you will ultimately find that you are afforded more freedom and peace of mind. And, after all, aren't those two of the most sought-after things in retirement?

An Additional Resource to Help You Keep Current

Tax rates, stock market performance and interest rates all change over time. As this book is being written, in January 2011, interest rates are currently at a 50-year low. Illustrations in this book reflect the current interest rate environment. I invite you to visit my website, www.boomersblueprint.com, which will update the material from this book and serve as an ongoing resource for you.

PART
ONE

CONSIDERATIONS IN CREATING
YOUR BLUEPRINT

1

TALKING 'BOUT MY GENERATION

In 2011, the leading edge of the Baby Boomers will turn 65. As more of the Boomers move into retirement, we will see greater numbers of retirees than ever before, as two generations (Boomers and their parents) will be retired at the same time. The Baby Boomers have made it a lifelong objective to distinguish themselves from their parents in just about everything they have done. Now, for the first time, they find themselves in the same stage of life as their parents: retirement. What will the retirement experience look like for the generation that reshaped the world?

Don't Stop 'til You Get Enough

Have you ever been driving to a destination and found yourself wondering if you had enough fuel to complete the trip? It is a very unsettling and stressful feeling and does not make for an enjoyable journey, for either the driver or the passenger(s). This same emotional distress and discomfort underlies a retiree's fear of running out of money. How enjoyable will retirement be if this is always front and centre as a concern or if every single decision has to be weighed carefully from a financial perspective?

The point here is to ensure that you are making the decision to retire from a position of financial confidence and comfort. There is not much merit in retiring if you have done so on such a restrictive budget that you cannot enjoy the lifestyle. This is why it's critical to have a formal income plan, or blueprint, show what your assets can realistically be expected to provide in terms of sustainable cash flow. After all, it is your cash flow that will fund your lifestyle. Granted, there are many things that change as one moves through retirement. Hence the need for reviewing, fine-tuning and occasionally redoing the blueprint. But one key to success is not retiring without adequate financial resources. Doing so can be a very unfortunate decision.

In several different ways, the Boomers have brought additional, self-imposed stress and uncertainty to their current or upcoming retirement experience because of their expectations. These must always be balanced by financial realities, but often this is not thought through carefully.

You may be mentally ready to retire but, as long as your state of health is not dictating your decision, you need to know that you are also financially ready and choose your timing accordingly. As is the case when building a house, the design and costs have to be in line with what you can afford. Simply stated, you wouldn't entertain putting up a house unless you knew the costs and had assessed if and how this would fit within your budget. If the costs were too high, then you might amend the design of your building to bring the cost of the project within budget. If your preference was to stick to the original design, then you might put off the project until such time as you had sufficient funding to do the job.

Deciding when to retire is similar. You can comfortably decide to retire *if*:

- you have sufficient assets and benefits to create the income you need to provide the lifestyle you want, and
- the income can be sustained throughout your retirement

Those are important requirements. If one of these is out of balance, you have some decisions to make. You could consider retiring into a somewhat more conservative and less expensive lifestyle. This would require less cash flow and could help to extend the life of your income-producing assets such that you can retire now. Another option would be to still focus on your original lifestyle objectives and simply work longer to build up additional retirement assets. It really does come down to a personal assessment because every situation is unique.

Everyone (and every couple) has their own:

- reasons for wanting to retire
- lifestyle objectives
- priorities and preferences
- cash flow needs and time frame
- income-producing assets and benefits to create income
- family issues
- state of health as they enter retirement

I am sure you have heard many general rules of thumb on the level of assets or income people need in retirement. Those opinions vary from "you must have at least a million dollars" to "government benefits will give you most of what you need" and everything in between. Do you need 70 per cent of your pre-retirement income as is often suggested? Well, that depends on the factors that are listed above. You may need more than 70 per cent or you may need less.

This is why you need to have a blueprint. It will allow you to design what you wish to do and understand the financing required to do it. From there it becomes a function of executing the plan and doing so in the most efficient manner possible.

Mama Told Me Not to Come

Hey, why didn't this retirement thing seem so tough for Mom and Dad? Was there something that they should have told us that they didn't? We Baby Boomers are supposed to be the advanced generation with new ideas and the ones who have everything under control. Yet it seems like retirement was easier and far less stressful for our parents. In reality, not all parents of Boomers had it easier in retirement, but there are differences between the generations.

Most of our parents worked at their job, career or business until they were 65. My father boasted that he was "retiring early," after 49 years of employment at the same firm, at the age of 64. And therein is a very important point. He worked for the *same* employer for all of his working years.

And while this is a common trait for the parents of the Boomers, it is seldom the situation for Boomers themselves. And this trend to many employers has steadily increased over the last 20 years. Often it is not the choice of the employee but a function of what is happening with the employer. The end result, however, is that many Boomers have found themselves leaving what had been longer-term employment in the critical period 10 to 12 years prior to their target retirement date. This normally would have been the prime earning and saving time within a familiar employment context.

Employment change at that juncture in life often results in a reduction in income and, correspondingly, in the amounts being put toward savings. New employers may not offer the same type of retirement programs, such as pensions or deferred profit sharing. These factors all contribute to an end scenario that is less attractive and less certain than the one our parents experienced. Most of our parents had only one or two employers through-out their working years. And while not every employer provided a pension plan, they were more prevalent than they are today, and a greater number of the pension plans were the more generous defined benefit programs.

Many Baby Boomers started their families later in life, and children are living at home longer than they ever have before. So the Boomers may not have had an empty nest as early as their parents did. Even if the Boomers did successfully launch their offspring, it is quite possible that one or more of the children have returned to the nest, perhaps with grandchildren in tow.

For the Boomers, the rate of divorce runs between 40 and 50 per cent. This is far higher than the experience of their parents. As anyone who has been through a divorce will tell you, in addition to the huge emotional toll there is a substantial financial cost. In many cases, this has disrupted the retirement savings and benefits that had accrued to that point. Remarriage and blended families also put pressure on financial resources.

Many Boomers find themselves in a situation where they are being pulled from several sides, with parents who need some help and/or care-giving, plus adult children, grandchildren or even a marital partner who also need support. It is a tug-of-war that involves emotions, time and money.

The distinctions between the lives of Boomers and of our parents do not make us inferior to our parents or mean that we have done a less-than-adequate job in preparing for retirement. You can't really draw accurate or valid comparisons between scenarios when there are so many variables.

My experience working with people through their retirement has shown that it can be, and usually is, a very rewarding time of life. My hope is to see people enjoying it to the fullest through all of its different phases. This can be achieved by finding the most efficient ways to use the assets clients have accumulated in order to create the cash flow to fund their retirement.

We Can Work It Out: *Transitioning*

Another possible course of action for those wanting to retire is what I refer to as "transitioning" into retirement. When you transition into retirement, you no longer work full-time but neither are you fully retired. It is a way to move gradually into a completely retired lifestyle.

There are several benefits to this approach: it provides you with an adjustment period, increases your personal time and enhances your financial position.

The Adjustment Period

As great as it is to have full discretion with your time, retirement is a new phase in one's life that is very different. Transitioning allows you an opportunity to make the adjustment from full-time employment to no employment gradually. While full retirement may not seem like a difficult thing to get used to, it is a major life change.

Personal Time

While there are many reasons people look forward to retiring, two of the more common motivators are: they want more discretion with their time or they are simply tired of the work they are doing. Transitioning may help address both of those issues. Obviously, working less creates more personal time. Becoming self-employed, or doing part-time, casual, contract or consulting work allows you to change the work you were doing. And it need not be with the same firm or even in the same occupation.

To that end, an increasingly intriguing aspect of transitioning is incorporating it into a strategy that is referred to as a "sustainable retirement lifestyle." Many people still look at retirement, to use a football analogy, with a "cross the goal line" mentality. They are going to work full-time to a certain point and then just stop and retire. That becomes their version of crossing the goal line. But in order to do that, they have to be sure that they have built sufficient assets to replace the employment income they have left behind. Well, they may not have saved enough by the time they had hoped to stop working. Or, as they near that end zone, the stock markets may have dragged down the value of their retirement assets. Either way, they find themselves in a situation where they have to keep working. Sometimes the goalposts and the end zone keep moving further into the future. And they may never get into that end zone if they keep moving the goalposts out for whatever reason.

A sustainable retirement lifestyle incorporates reduced work with expanded leisure and gets rid of that "either/or" thinking. When you look at how the work week comes together for most people, they have five days of work and two days off. One of those two days is going to be dedicated to chores that need to get done, such as buying groceries, mowing the lawn et cetera. That leaves one day that is fully discretionary. When people think of retirement, they think of every day as being fully discretionary. But it doesn't have to be so black or white. If you cut your work week down to four days, look what happens: you still have to do the same household chores, but you now have two days where you have full discretion. That is twice the time for yourself than you had before. A three-day work week would create three days for you to do what you want to do. It does not have to be all or nothing.

Your Financial Position

A dollar of employment income is a dollar that you don't have to take from your retirement assets. You may not be adding to your savings, but if your reduced employment income fully satisfies your cash flow needs, you have allowed your income-producing assets additional time to grow in value. You may need a blend of employment income and personal assets to make this work. That is still beneficial, because at the end of the day you are still taking less from your assets than you would be without employment income.

Transitioning is particularly valuable when an individual has a desire to leave his or her current employment but, from a financial standpoint, does not feel comfortable doing so. The decision to work or to retire does not have to be a choice between black and white. There are many shades of grey, which, when you think about it, is very appropriate for the retirement crowd.

You're Going to Carry That Weight: *Taking Debt into Retirement*

Our parents seemed very willing to make do with what they had and live within their means. There are very few Boomers out there who have not heard at least one story about how frugally and carefully their parents handled money or did without. In fact, this still holds true for how they live and spend in their retirement. This is mirrored in comical scenes from *Seinfeld*, where Jerry's parents, retired in Florida, rush to have supper at 4:30 in order to catch the less costly "early-bird special."

But not so the Baby Boom generation. We are masters of spending not only what we earn but even more than we earn. Thank goodness for credit, a tool our parents may have used for buying a house but not for many other purchases. But how would we, as Boomers, ever be able to keep up with our friends and relatives in terms of possessions or experiences if we weren't able to buy now and pay later? For many Boomers, this was simply the way it was done, and we managed to find new ways to get more credit and more possessions. Credit allowed us to create a lifestyle pattern where we could continually consume more than we could afford. As a result, a lot of Baby Boomers did things when they wanted to rather than when they should have.

But retirement, and funding it, is totally different. In order to retire, we have to pay first and enjoy later. This is contrary to how Boomers have done most things throughout their working life. You can't borrow to fund your retirement. That must be paid for in advance. You can really only consider retiring when you can afford to, not simply when you want to. It is a decision driven more by financial reality than by desire.

A retirement survey conducted in 2010 by RBC uncovered that four in ten retirees had some form of debt when they retired and nearly one in four had a mortgage on their primary residence. The issue here is that servicing a mortgage or a debt is a drain on cash flow that would otherwise be used to fund lifestyle in retirement. Chapter 8 touches on this issue in more detail. That said, I have also had clients tell me that the decision to take on new debt or a mortgage in retirement is part of their lifestyle objectives. As an example, if the expectation after retirement is to spend more time in their home, they may feel that servicing a loan needed for making renovations or improvements is a very valid lifestyle expenditure.

Ideally, you want to be debt free at the time you actually retire. There is a great deal of comfort, satisfaction and security in having everything "paid for." This is not to say that you can't retire or you should not retire if you are servicing debt. But the fact is, you will have to dedicate income toward servicing that debt. And that is cash flow that could be used to enhance your lifestyle in other ways. In addition, a certain dollar amount or percentage of your income-producing assets is also going to be tied up, producing the income required for your payments.

You also need to be aware of how taxes impact your non-deductible debt. Table 1.1 shows what a loan looks like if your income falls within the first two federal tax brackets (2011).

TABLE 1.1: The Tax-Adjusted Cost of a Loan

Loan Rate	Your Pre-Tax Rate, Income of <$41,545	Your Pre-Tax Rate, Income of >$41,544
4.0%	5.40%	6.24%
5.0%	6.74%	7.80%
6.0%	8.10%	9.36%

So if you have taxable income in 2011 that is above $41,544, servicing a loan with a 5 per cent interest rate with after-tax money is going to require a fully-taxable source of income equal to 7.80 per cent. That could represent more strain on your retirement assets than you think.

The preceding points comparing the Baby Boom generation to our parents are not at all intended to slight anyone. They simply emphasize that situations are different today. But isn't that what the Baby Boom generation has wanted all along—to differentiate ourselves from our parents? And in being different we need to look at retirement issues and solutions that are different from our parents'. Your blueprint is not going to be the same as your parents'. It can't be, unless you are expecting that your retirement is going to be exactly the same as theirs. But I have not run into many Baby Boomers who feel that way. So you better start getting your own distinctive blueprint pulled together based on what *you* are hoping to experience in your retirement.

MAKING YOUR BLUEPRINT WORK FOR YOU

1. Don't make the decision to retire without knowing that you have the assets you need to fund the lifestyle you seek. This is one of the prime functions of your blueprint. It can help you determine if it is feasible to do what you want on what you have. Retiring too early, with inadequate financial resources may free you from a work situation you are anxious to leave, but often results in a more stressful experience from which you cannot extract yourself.

2. Your retirement is not going to look like Mom and Dad's retirement. Having realistic expectations is one of the key factors in enjoying a fulfilling experience. Have you (and more importantly, you and your spouse) defined your expectations for what you want out of retirement and have you shared them with each other? You need to think through the design you want for your own retirement and have a blueprint drafted to address that design. Your blueprint will help you to get the most out of your time and your assets going forward.

3. Your retirement lifestyle may involve working, for any one of a number of reasons. This may not necessarily be where you worked up to the point of retirement and may not even be connected to what you did through your working years.

4. Remember that carrying debt into retirement is very different from the approach our parents took, but it is not uncommon for Boomers. You are not going to "burn in hell" for retiring with a loan or mortgage. But you do need to realize that servicing any indebtedness in retirement is going to require a commitment from retirement cash flow and the assets that create that cash flow.

2

KEY CONCEPTS FOR AN
EFFICIENT BLUEPRINT

When building a house, a great deal of thought and planning must go into general considerations for the project as a whole. There will be some basic things that have been decided first, such as the type of house, location on the lot, possession date et cetera. This is done well in advance of the design and blueprint phase.

In a similar way, before we can move on to actually drafting your blueprint, it is necessary for you to understand some of the basic concepts of income planning as well as some of the keys to making most efficient use of your retirement assets.

The Four Planning Channels

There are four distinct planning channels involved in comprehensive retirement income planning. They are:

1. The Structural Plan
2. The Investment Portfolio
3. Health-Risk Management
4. Wealth Transfer

These channels work together in the same way as framing, electrical, plumbing and heating do in a home.

Each of these channels is a process unto itself. Because each time a decision is reached and action is taken in one of the planning areas it affects the other three, the true benefits of integrated planning will only be realized when all four work in conjunction. For example, an increase in the amount of income withdrawn (structure) will reduce potential inheritances (wealth transfer), and may affect the ability to fund long-term health-care costs (health-risk management), unless the investments (investment portfolio) are adjusted to attract a potentially higher rate of return.

In my last book, *Buying Time*, I examined all four of these planning channels and the relationships between them. However, the purpose of this book is to emphasize the efficient delivery of income throughout your retirement. As such, the focus will be on the first two channels, the structural plan and the investment portfolio. However, I will touch on health-risk management as part of overall risk management. This is an important issue for the Baby Boomers and will become increasingly so as they move forward through their retirement.

Your Architect and Your Contractor

You need both an architect to create your plan and a contractor to implement it. I have found that things work most efficiently when your planner also has involvement in and/or oversight of the management of the income-producing assets. First let's talk about using an advisor as the architect of your blueprint.

In 2005, a major report was produced and issued to the member companies of the Life Insurance Marketing and Research Association (LIMRA). The report focused on the needs of consumers who were either in retirement or were a few years away from commencing retirement. It spelled out the need for member companies to get their advisors properly trained in order to be able to assist their clients in making the transition from the accumulation year to the income years.

And therein is a very interesting point. Over the last two decades, there has been much emphasis from financial institutions and advisors on helping people accumulate the assets that, in turn, would serve to provide income in retirement. And that was a very appropriate focus at the time. But as the Baby Boomers came closer to retirement, a shift began to happen and is still unfolding. People need help in turning these assets into income and advisors who are proficient in this specific area are not all that easy to find. In fact, the conclusion of the LIMRA report, referring to those people who are about to commence retirement income, was this: "People need advice from a knowledgeable professional more at this point than at any other time in their life."

A qualified advisor is your architect in drafting your blueprint for retirement income. Using an advisor can be a significant factor in both successful planning and the resulting execution of the plan . . . but only if you are working with one who is truly knowledgeable in the area of retirement income planning. How do you find such a person?

I want to go on record as saying that there are some really great financial advisors who can help you in this area of retirement income planning. The first issue is that you need to find them among a vast number of advisors, the majority of whom can't help you efficiently. This is not a slight; it is really more a function of the fact that financial advisors tend either to be generalists or to focus on certain areas of business. You likely won't get the detailed help you need from a generalist, and you need to make sure that the advisor you are using does have a primary focus on this area of retirement income planning. Allow me a comparative example. I have a fabulous doctor who is a general practitioner. If I required heart surgery, I would rather that it be done be a specialist, with all due respect to my regular doctor who is a generalist. A heart surgeon and a gynecologist are both medical doctors and are both specialists. But I don't want a gynecologist, no matter how skilled, performing open heart surgery on me.

Just because you may have accumulated your retirement assets with an advisor or an institution doesn't mean they are necessarily your best choice when the time comes to transition to the withdrawal years. Basically, all of my clients had previously worked with another advisor or institution before I created a blueprint for them. This is a relatively new area of financial planning, and planning for the withdrawal years is a different art and science from planning for the accumulation years.

Do your own research when searching for an advisor. You may ask people you know for recommendations, but do your own due diligence to determine if what they do and who they are fit with what you want done and who you are. Of course there are the basic things that you want to know from the "find an advisor checklist," such as their professional designations, experience, liability coverage et cetera. In addition, you may also want to include the following in assessing an advisor:

- Can they show you what it is they do?
- What do their written plans (blueprints) look like?
- What are the processes they employ for structuring income and the investment portfolios that will provide that income?
- Can they help you address the additional aspects of health-risk management and wealth transfer?

The second part of this section deals with your contractor. By this I mean the person who oversees the investments that create income from your assets. It should be the same person as your architect, and if not, there should be a direct working relationship between the two. It may be one person or a team of people who specialize, but the blueprint and oversight of the use of your assets has to be in sync. The investments used may be mutual funds, investment pools, ETFs, GICs, individual stocks and bonds or any combination of those instruments. The key point is that there has to be coordination between your invested assets and the execution of the plan. There are different ways in which this can be set up, including the following:

- Your planner may choose and manage the investments for you.
- Your planner may refer you to a private investment counsel but still "quarterback" the entire process.
- Your investment advisor may have "in-house" planners who create the blueprint for you.

This is not solely about creating the blueprint to detail how your income should be created. Nor is this solely about how your money is invested. It is about the two of these things working in tandem. Otherwise, the creation of your income and the use of your assets cannot be executed efficiently.

It may become apparent to you that it is in your best interest to make a change from your current advisor or institution, and this will mean moving your investments to another planner. While this occurs in the industry every day, it is likely not something you have done often. As the saying goes, "breaking up is hard to do," and while you may feel a bit awkward about ending a relationship with your existing planner, remember that this is not about them. It is about you and what you feel is in your best interest. No advisor likes to lose a client. But you do need to coordinate the planning with the investments, and if this can be done in a better way for you elsewhere, then you should seriously consider making a move.

Remember, and this is critical, I am not referring here to *retirement* planning, which many advisors say they do. I am specifically referring to *retirement income* planning, and that art and science is effectively practised by very few at this point in time.

One last point on this topic. It may be your desire to handle your retirement planning on your own, and that is certainly an option. Remember, however, that this is not solely about managing investments. Far from it. Please know that my recommendation to work with an advisor is not in any way to suggest that you are inept or unable. But I am convinced that people are better served over time by using the services of a professional to help them along this journey. I have found that in most cases where people choose to do this on their own, there eventually comes a time when either it will no longer be of interest or they start to feel uncomfortable with being fully capable of handling their own affairs.

Come Together: Consolidating Your Assets

The decision to find and work with an advisor who can help meet your unique income planning needs at this time in your life is an important first step. But there is also another essential purpose for this. Experience has shown repeatedly that there is particular merit in coordinating all of your planning activities with one person or institution. I refer to it as "consolidation," and it delivers more effective planning and better results for you.

When you are accumulating the savings and assets that will ultimately be used to create your retirement income, you may be doing this in several different locations and be using more than one advisor. Part of the asset building may also be happening through plans that you have at your place of employment. This may result in less-than-perfect asset allocation for you, but, other than that, there is not really much downside.

However, when the time comes to withdraw retirement income from those assets, you cannot have complete efficiency if you have things scattered about at various institutions. If you are married or have a partner, then you both need to have things pulled together. It all has to do with controlling cash flow and taxes, and this cannot be done efficiently unless all of the household investments are consolidated.

Think of it this way: Imagine someone goes to a doctor. Although the patient describes what is causing his discomfort, he does not tell the doctor everything. The doctor writes out a prescription based on what she has been told and what she believes to be the appropriate course of action. Then the patient immediately meets with another doctor in the next building and describes the rest of his symptoms, but doesn't mention anything he explained to the first doctor. That second physician also issues a prescription to address what he believes to be the problem.

This is inefficient because neither physician knows the whole story and the solutions they prescribe might be very different if they were aware of all of the details. Will the medications conflict with or counteract each other? What were the other recommendations to the patient and are those at cross-purposes? In this example, was the person better served by visiting two physicians and only sharing with each of them part of the story?

Making best use of your income goes hand in hand with making best use of your assets. And that can only happen if you consolidate them with one advisor or institution. Having things scattered about between competing advisors is not a form of efficient diversification. Consolidating your assets affords you the following benefits:

- better planning, no conflicting advice, less confusion
- more control over amounts and sources of income
- more efficient asset allocation/better portfolios

- more opportunity for tax-efficiency/savings
- less administration (reporting, number of cheques)
- the potential for higher deposit rates
- access to enhanced investment options and lower fee structures
- more orderly, expedient and less costly wealth transfer (easier for surviving spouse, beneficiaries and estate)

Of course, any advisor or institution would like to attract all of your investment capital. Yes, they will gain by having all of your business, but you will be the much larger beneficiary of such action. You cannot achieve the same degree of efficiency for the benefits listed above unless you consolidate your holdings.

One concern you may have is that moving certain non-registered investments may create some taxable capital gains. Moving does not necessarily mean selling the investment, or "cashing things in." A change of servicing agent and the ability to move investments to another advisor or institution in kind, meaning "as they are," will allow the change to be made without creating a taxable disposition.

I'm Your Handyman: Fixing the Inefficiencies That Cost You

When I speak of inefficiencies or weaknesses, I am not suggesting that things won't work if they are set up improperly. What I am pointing out is that things could function in a much better and more efficient fashion. As an example, it is like when a client is driving to my office for a meeting. She could have the gear shift set in "drive" or she could make the trip in first gear. Either way, she will get to my office. But if she drove the car in first gear:

- it would take longer
- it would cost more because of the amount of additional fuel being used
- it would put unnecessary strain on the vehicle she is using

And she could have reached the same destination far more efficiently simply by having the gear shift in "drive." Over and over again I meet

people for the first time and see that their income-producing assets are being "driven in first gear." There is needless waste and strain on their assets
because their cash flow is not being created efficiently. A properly designed
blueprint can dramatically reduce and even negate the waste and the inefficiencies present in so many situations.

Earlier in this chapter, I put forward the contention that there are very
few advisors who are truly proficient in the area of retirement income
planning and that you need to find one who is. The emphasis for most
advisors is still on investments and other financial products, not on the
planning aspects that are so important to creating income efficiently. While
investments and financial products do have a meaningful role as tools in
executing the blueprint, I often find a collection of products without any
type of plan or process involved.

Generally speaking, what I see in these situations is that consumers
are being:

- ineptly advised
- underserviced
- overcharged

Some of the opportunities for improvement that commonly arise include
the following:

- preserving government benefits and entitlements
- preserving tax credits
- reducing taxes payable on income and on estate transfer
- reducing investment costs and improving returns
- putting less strain on income-producing assets to create the
  income needed
- enhancing wealth-transfer opportunities for heirs and charities
- using insurance vehicles for health-risk management and wealth
  transfer

It is significant to note that you will benefit *every year* from improvements that are made to your situation. As such, there is a cumulative

benefit that will be realized over an extended number of years, the value of which would flow from this formula:

$$\text{the value of your income-producing assets}$$
$$X$$
$$\text{the number of years you (or you and your spouse) are retired}$$
$$=$$
$$\text{a very meaningful dollar amount}$$

This is all part of asset conservation and overall wealth management. Throughout the balance of this book, I will identify the most common inefficiencies and also discuss how to improve them. In doing so, I hope to be able to more clearly illustrate where there are opportunities for improvement in most situations.

Throughout this chapter, I have repeated my belief that there is not a large number of financial advisors who are specialized and proficient in the area of creating retirement income. This is not intended to be a slight or a criticism of the industry, nor am I trying to "beat up" on financial advisors. After all, I am an advisor and I do a great deal of retirement income planning training work with them, either through corporate consulting or at conferences and workshops. The industry is evolving and the number of advisors who choose to focus on retirement income planning is growing. My intention is to encourage you to make sure that the person with whom you are working can deliver what will help you to make best use of your money and your time throughout your retirement years. You have taken a lifetime to accumulate the income-producing assets that you have. You deserve to get the most from what they can deliver for you, both in terms of income and satisfaction, and to do so with minimum waste and maximum efficiency.

On and On: The Income Continuum

The last of the key concepts is the "Income Continuum." It is a simple yet important consideration in the initial and evolving development of your blueprint. The objective of the continuum is to deliver the cash flow you need in the best possible way throughout your retirement. This includes:

1. delivering tax-efficient income as retirement begins
2. being aware of how decisions made today, in terms of which assets to use, will impact how income is created in the future
3. ensuring adequate and favourably positioned income for a surviving spouse or partner (if applicable)
4. transitioning remaining assets to the estate in the most tax-effective way

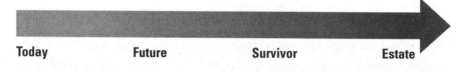

Today   **Future**   **Survivor**   **Estate**

Yes, your blueprint will need to be adjusted when life-altering events move you into another stage of your retired life (see Chapter 3, Step 1). Part of retirement income planning involves understanding that it is not a static event. It is not a case of setting up sources of income at the outset and letting things run from there. It is a hands-on progression that requires, at the very least, an annual review to determine how income should be created on a year-to-year basis.

In retirement, your income will come from a variety of sources, including government benefits, personal assets, pension and possibly income from employment. The strategy of combining these various sources of income in an efficient and logical manner is referred to as "layering." The actual layering of your various income sources is something that should be revisited and reviewed every year. Your blueprint will lay out the general strategy and emphasize the most effective use of these sources over the longer term. This is why a long-term relationship with an advisor is best and why asset management goes hand in hand with the planning role.

MAKING YOUR BLUEPRINT WORK FOR YOU

1. This book focuses on two of the four distinct planning channels: creating the blueprint or written plan and employing the related investment tools, approaches and strategies. The objective is to help you to "intelligently disassemble" what you have taken a lifetime to accumulate.

2. If your current advisor or planner cannot produce a detailed written retirement income plan (blueprint), then you may want to find someone else with whom to work in order to more effectively address the specific needs you have at this particular time in your life. The person or team with whom you are working needs to have oversight of the investments and the execution of the plan so things work in tandem.

3. It is important at this point in your life to bring together all of the different personal assets you have scattered about with different institutions and advisors.

4. It is through these combined actions that you will have the best opportunity to minimize the inefficiencies that occur in so many retirement income situations.

5. Use the Income Continuum to create your income efficiently throughout your retirement.

PART
TWO

BUILDING YOUR INCOME PLAN
WITH THE SIX-STEP PLAN

3

LAYING THE FOUNDATION FOR YOUR INCOME PLAN

The Six-Step Plan is a process that I have used for over 20 years and serves as a template for creating your blueprint. The use of this income planning process provides a consistent experience for you regardless of where you happen to be in your retirement life cycle. It is also a template that you can use for review and revision.

The steps are as follows:

1. assessing your current life stage
2. establishing your lifestyle and time objectives
3. determining your financial goals and priorities
4. creating the income needed through layering
5. aligning your investments with your income plan
6. assessing the impact of the plan on your net worth

Your Role in the Design

The process has to start with you. You are the one who must design what you want your retirement to look like. Your detailed input is required. The architect and contractor who will put together and implement your blueprint can't just make it up out of thin air and have it be meaningful or appropriate for you. However, your advisor will be able to let you know if what you wish to do fits within what can be provided and sustained by your financial resources. Yes, things will change over time, just as buildings may have alterations, renovations or additions as time goes on. But at the outset, they are still built based on a basic design, and so it should be with planning your retirement and merging your time with your money.

Obviously, there are shorter-term lifestyle and financial objectives that are easier to articulate, but some thought should be put into the mid-term and longer-term horizons as well. In addition to your financial details, your advisor needs to know your wants, needs, concerns, preferences and values. Based in their knowledge, experience and insight, they can then put forward a detailed course of action aimed at enabling you to fulfill your objectives. This is another reason why it is critical for you to find someone who is qualified to do this specific kind of work for you.

Pulling all of the necessary information together is not a 10-minute exercise. Doing this properly is going to take some thought, some time and some effort. The more you put in up front, the better and more meaningful your blueprint will be. As a tool to assist you and your advisor in the planning process, I want to provide access to the data-gathering forms I use in my practice. They list the information that an advisor will need in order to provide you with a customized retirement income blueprint. The forms are available for you to download and print at www.boomersblueprint.com.

Step 1. Assessing Your Current Life Stage

One of the key things to be aware of when planning the use of your time and your assets in retirement is that it is not a static event. It is not a case of setting up the blueprint and then having things simply running according to plan from that point forward. Retirement income planning is a process.

Stages in Retirement

You may ultimately spend from one-quarter to one-half of your adult life in retirement. I refer to this period of time as your "retirement life cycle." It is very common for people to think of retirement as one phase in life, when in fact it comprises many different stages over a 20- to 40-year period.

Some of these stages include:

- positioning yourself to begin your retirement
- starting your retirement
- the early or prime years of retirement
- children returning home—the not-so-empty nest
- arrival of grandchildren
- changes in your health
- disability or failing health of a spouse or partner
- caring for adult children
- caring for aging parents
- changing your place of residence or type of accommodation
- breakdown of marriage
- death of friends
- loss of a spouse or partner

Most of the stages identified above tend to involve health-related events, changes in family situation and sometimes both. I refer to these as "life-altering events" because what follows will always be different from what preceded these events. It is important to note that the vast majority of retirees will go through any number of these events in their lifetime. These events can and do occur before retirement, but most are typically associated with aging. These are retirement realities and they need to be recognized when setting objectives and considering how to use your assets, health-risk management and wealth transfer.

The fact that these changes will impact your situation is one of the reasons why I emphasize using an advisor. Adapting to the changes that these events will bring is much easier and more efficient for you if you have a blueprint in place and someone with whom you can discuss it. The main reason to use an advisor is because the creation of a blueprint is not what makes things happen. It is the *implementation* of the blueprint that makes things happen. Your advisor's role should also include assisting you to take the steps necessary to put the plan into action and turn your objectives into reality. Your relationship with your advisor, and the role he or she plays, will constantly change, just as your needs change through the various stages of retirement.

There is a different set of planning parameters that applies once you move from the accumulation years to the income years. In the accumulation years, you know how to define what you want. For example, you can tell a planner your target retirement date, the amount of income you want at that time, how much you can save between now and then et cetera. You can also provide all of the financial information regarding what you have accumulated to date. An advisor can then work through what needs to be saved at an expected rate of return, with the goal of having you get to where you want to be by the time you want to be there.

When income commences, the value of your assets and the monthly income you wish to have are the "knowns" in the situation. What neither you nor your advisor know is how long that income will have to be paid out. It could be 3 months or 43 years. There are no defined planning parameters around good health or longevity. This is why health-risk management differs greatly from the accumulation years to the income years. In the income years, the loss of health or death are no longer simply possibilities, but eventualities. And that is a very different risk-management discussion compared to the years when assets are being built.

So your first step is to recognize what stage you are at in your retirement life cycle. One of the key benefits of using this planning template to create your blueprint is that no matter what stage you happen to be at as you initiate this, it is the same Six-Step Plan that is used repeatedly.

Step 2. Establishing Your Lifestyle and Time Objectives: The Time Hub

In my previous publication, *Buying Time*, I used the term "Time Hub" to encompass the lifestyle planning issues and the use of one's time in retirement. I will continue to do so in this book. I use the word "hub" as a description because these considerations are always changing. They are dynamic, contracting, expanding and evolving from what were the central considerations at the outset. And this continues to happen as you move through retirement.

Your Time Hub is composed of your key personal needs and your objectives, including what you wish to do with your time. And there are many things, including people, that will affect your decisions in this area. The priorities within this hub are driven by a combination of emotional, psychological and physical well-being. They cover a number of different areas of importance. And each one of them has financial implications, as well.

Often, the retirement income planning exercise focuses only on what the income needs are. For example, "How much income do you need to have each month?" True, it is necessary to know this, and the planning process requires that this be identified and provided to your advisor to help put your financial plan together. But what are the factors that have driven the need for this level of income at this point in time? It is more than just a numerical calculation. It is necessary to think through some other key questions that are part of the Time Hub priorities and considerations and include the following:

- How are you feeling about retirement?
  I have spoken to people who were actually crossing off the days on their calendar to get to their retirement date. I have also met people who were quite frightened by the thought of not having the structure of going to work. How do you feel about your retirement?

- What role, if any, will work play in your retirement plans?
  Maintaining some form of employment seems to be the evolving and expanding trend with retiring Boomers for a number of different reasons. Work may be part of your plan as you transition into retirement. How much of your time would you dedicate to this? What form would it take—seasonal, part-time, contract, casual or consulting? Is there a particular type of work that you would like? Volunteer work also fits into this area.

- What activities will you engage in to maintain your physical and mental well-being?
  If your response is simply "keep busy," then you had better think this through in a little bit more detail. What specific

activities will you engage in or continue to pursue when you are
in your retirement?

- What are your family priorities and/or issues?

  Often people don't consider how their retirement may impact
  other family members or, conversely, how other family members
  may impact their retirement. As an example, as wonderful as
  togetherness is, how will you and your spouse adjust to spending all of your time together once you are both retired? Adult
  children returning home, aging parents needing some help or
  both may take up some of that time you thought you were going
  to have for your own pursuits. Family issues may also infringe
  on your finances.

- Where will you reside?

  There are potentially two parts to that question. First, do you
  plan to stay in the same city or town you are in now or will
  you move away? Will that move take you closer to children or
  closer to a warmer climate or to a change in lifestyle? Second,
  are you planning to stay in the same type of residence that you
  are in currently? How might where you live change as you move
  through your retirement?

- How will you deal with changes in your health or in that of your
  spouse?

  It is inevitable that as you move through your retirement years
  your health is going to decline. It is not a fun thing to think
  about, but it is an important reality to recognize. And it may be
  your health or the health of your partner that is involved, but
  it will introduce changes in what you either can do or wish to
  do. Those changes may be very minor or quite limiting. They
  are going to happen, and you can't control them. All you can
  control is how you react, adjust and deal with them.

- How do you view spending your time?

    What are your lifestyle and fulfillment goals? What do you plan to do? What are the things you enjoy doing now that you will have more time to pursue? What are some of the new and different interests you want to investigate now that you will have the time? Keeping active and not having "watching TV" as your number one activity ties in directly with keeping physically and mentally healthy. You need to think through what you are going to do with your time once you have more discretion with it. If you are already retired, you may have fulfilling things that you are doing with your time currently, and that is great. If this is not the case, what can you do to make better and more satisfying use of your time from this point forward? There is a very appropriate question that needs to be addressed by anyone approaching retirement, or, for that matter, already in it. It may sound trite, but it is this: "You know what you are retiring from, but do you know what you are retiring to?"

Other Time Hub Considerations

- In addition to financial plans, what other plans have you made?
- If you had all the money you could ever use or want, what are the first five things that you would do, and why?
- What are the 10 things you want to do while your health permits? What is their order of priority for you, and what is the time frame within which you want to accomplish each of them?

The last point mentioned above is really important. If you can set up a list of priorities and a time frame within which you would like to accomplish them, you stand a much better chance of actually doing them. The more specific you can be in creating this list, the better. Financing certain objectives will likely require income or capital that may be in addition to the normal monthly cash flow you require. You will need to budget for this in Step 3.

Time Hub priorities are not measured per se, but rather are defined. Identifying the priorities in this area, as is evident from the questions you need to consider, is really a subjective exercise. You will need to invest some thought and effort to accurately answer the Time Hub questions. If you are married, it is very possible that the Time Hub priorities, objectives and attitudes may differ greatly between you and your partner. It is important that you work through this exercise together to address your combined needs. In fact, you may find it both revealing and rewarding for each of you to go through the Time Hub priorities on the data-gathering forms and the questions listed here on your own—and then compare notes. This will let you know how closely your own vision of retirement is aligned with that of your partner. You will likely find that there are some things common, some differences and some surprises, especially if there is a large difference in age. That is what makes it a very worthwhile exercise.

Once your lifestyle and time priorities have been defined, they need to be reflected on the financial side of the blueprint, where things can be quantified as part of your budgeting process. Stated another way, the Time Hub priorities define the "what," and the Money Hub (Step 3) facilitates the "how." Until you define your Time Hub priorities, you can't accurately determine how much income you will need. In my opinion and from my experience, you need to know the regular cash flow you will require before you can properly determine how to invest your income-producing assets. The objective is to have your Time Hub and Money Hub working in tandem through your blueprint. You are not going to know all of the answers for your entire retirement right at this moment. As I have said previously, that is because things are constantly changing during this period of your life. But you need to have a very good picture of what you want to do now and give some thought to future plans. The vast majority of Baby Boomers coming into retirement agree that their retirement will look very different from the one that their parents enjoyed. Yet, for the vast majority of Boomers, what they have seen their parents go through is the only comprehensive frame of reference that they have on the subject. Since their own retirement is not going to be the same as their parents', they had better develop a clear and defined picture of what it is going to look like.

And how, exactly, will your priorities change over two or three decades of retirement? Other than to say that there will be many changes and different stages, this is really the unknown. That is why I feel strongly that when creating income from assets, the structure should be flexible enough to allow for changes in priorities throughout these stages. Take the example of two couples about to commence their retirement: they are both the same ages, with the same retirement assets and income potential. How would the Time Hub factors, priorities and objectives differ between these two couples if the husband in one family had just been diagnosed with a life-threatening illness?

Or, consider two people who are retired. One is 63 and has just spent her first month of retirement in a sunny, tropical location. The other is 83 and has just lost her partner after 55 years of marriage. How do their views of retirement differ? What are their views of the future? How would their Time Hub and, subsequently, their Money Hub priorities differ? Going back to Step 1, they are definitely at different stages in their respective retirements. Part of this exercise of planning for your lifestyle in retirement is to help you make the best use of your prime retirement years. I define the "prime retirement years" as that period of time from the commencement of your retirement, in whatever manner you engage in it, to that point in time where you or your spouse needs care or passes away. Whether you retire at age 52, 62 or 72, the first 10 years of your retirement will likely be the most fulfilling. This is because these are usually the years in which you and your spouse will enjoy the best health during your retirement. This is the time that is referred to as the "golden years." When health fails or a partner passes away, you may find yourself in the "olden years."

By defining more precisely what it is that you wish to do in your best retirement years, both time and financial resources can be used in the most meaningful and efficient manner. I have met people of varying ages who waited to do the things they wanted to do and then lost their health, or worse, their partner. It is a shame that some people don't make the best use of their time or the wealth they have built. The beneficiaries of this overly frugal behaviour are usually their heirs and the tax department—and not the individuals themselves.

Step 3. Determining Your Financial Goals and Priorities: The Money Hub

The Money Hub pertains to those assets, benefits and entitlements that will be used to create income and to the priorities you attach to their use. It also includes very important decisions about the level of retirement income you want or need to create. The Money Hub can be objectively and technically planned once the advisor knows your lifestyle and income needs. So while this part of your blueprint does focus on income, the Money Hub also addresses the use of your assets generating that cash flow.

Changes to Cash Flow at Retirement

Okay, this is it! This is your last day at work. Just before you leave, you are handed your final paycheque. What are some of the differences in expenditures you will experience when you are transitioning from employment to retirement? If you are already retired, you are very familiar with some of these issues. Some of the changes that occur are subtle and gradual, some are obvious and immediate. Either way, there is an impact—financially, psychologically or both. These are issues with which you should be familiar. Some of the more noticeable changes are listed below.

- Costs related to work disappear. Transportation costs, clothing specific to work, and the cost of meals or lunches are no longer a factor.
- Group insurance benefits (disability and life insurance) are commonly terminated or at least reduced when someone leaves an employer. A key planning point to examine is which, if any, of these benefits may be appropriate to continue on an individual basis. Health considerations also enter into this decision. Someone in poor health may very well want to take advantage of the non-medical conversion options for life insurance coverage available in group plans.
- With the departure from employee benefit programs, the costs of dental care, some medical requirements and prescription drugs now fall to the individual. These costs have the potential to be quite high.

- While working, it is typical for people to spend most of their discretionary money on weekends and holidays, which is really leisure time. In retirement, a person has 100 per cent leisure time.
- As you go through your working years, you receive a regular paycheque from your employer. Retirement income, however, is created from benefits and from making withdrawals from your own assets. This is a big change in how the creation of income occurs and is a large psychological shift.
- At the time an individual is no longer earning employment income, he or she is basically finished saving money. The process now becomes one of drawing income rather than accumulating assets. This may be the point in time when an individual has the greatest net worth. Part of the overall strategy in income planning is to preserve as much of that net worth as possible as you go through years of drawing income.
- When you are in receipt of retirement income, you are now responsible for making sure that there is sufficient tax being deducted and remitted from the various sources. This is explained in detail in Chapter 9.

It's Net Income That Counts

So you are looking at retiring and thinking, "Wow, how am I going to be able to replace my employment income?" Let's assume that between your government benefits and other income streams you can sustainably create from your personal assets a pre-tax retirement income of $4,000 per month. But your pre-tax employment income was $6,000 per month. That is a $2,000 per month difference, or 33 per cent per month less! Well, it is on a pre-tax basis anyway. That difference between your gross employment income and gross retirement income may appear quite significant. Some analysis of your earnings statement may narrow this disparity. Compare what you are bringing home on a net basis with what your net income will be in retirement. You may find the difference in net pay is not as significant as you thought. Here is a simple example using the above numbers and comparing net incomes before and after age 65 on a monthly basis.

TABLE 3.1 Difference in Incomes Before and After Retirement

	Employment Income	Retirement Income < Age 65	Difference	Retirement Income ≥ Age 65	Difference
Gross Income	$6,000	$4,000	-33.33%	$4,000	-33%
Income Tax	$1,237	$679		$649	
CPP Deduction	$185	0		0	
E.I. Premiums	$65	0		0	
Group Benefits	$213	0		0	
Pension at 4.5%	$270	0		0	
Group RRSP	$250	0		0	
Net Income	$3,780	$3,321	-12.14%	$3,351	11.35–10.64%

So the actual difference in the net monthly payment is not a reduction of 33 per cent but closer to 12.14 per cent (less after age 65). Stated another way: in this example, the retirement income is 87.86 per cent of the employment take-home pay. Your employment earnings have deductions for CPP, EI, retirement savings and benefit contributions, although most of these are deductible. This fact, combined with a higher rate of marginal tax on a larger portion of employment income, brings the two net income numbers more closely in line. The example for age 65 and over also includes the age credit in the calculation of tax payable, which has the effect of raising the net retirement income.

Setting Your Income Target

The closer you get to an actual retirement date, the more specifically you will be able to define the amount of income you will need. If you are already retired, then you have a very good idea of how this works. Income planning is more than totalling the sum of receipts from all sources. There are considerations of asset preservation, tax efficiency and inflation protection that must be addressed. But the first item of business to address in Step 3 is determining the amount of after-tax cash flow you need to come into your household every month.

Here is how I help clients and potential clients arrive at this number, and it works very effectively regardless of where they might be in their retirement life cycle. It simply involves working from a budget to determine the cash flow they will need. Admit it, you winced the very moment you read the word "budget." And that happened because you associate "budget" with other fun words such as "diet" and "celibacy." All three of these words carry a connotation of sacrifice or doing without in one way or another. That is not the intent here. The purpose of working through the budget is not to restrict you in any way, but to get an accurate number for what has to be funded by your retirement income.

This is why it is so important to think through some of the lifestyle and Time Hub issues in advance of getting to this point. Your decisions in that area do have an impact on what you are going to need for your income in retirement. Most of the lifestyle expenses tend to be the more discretionary items. On the budgeting form that I use with clients (illustrated on the next page), I have taken the step of distinguishing cash flow needs from cash flow wants (discretionary). Again, the budget form is available to you among the data-gathering forms that you can access at www.boomersblueprint.com.

This is a worthwhile exercise whether or not you are currently retired. If you are retired, you can do this to see what, if any, cash flow you may be wasting each month. This is done by comparing the total cash flow estimates from your budget page to your actual income. You may also find that there are areas where you are spending more than you originally thought. For those just about to leave employment and join the ranks of the retired, I suggest that you do a comparative check. Examine your pay stub, which shows your income and deductions, and look specifically at your take-home pay. How does that amount compare to what you are projecting as your retirement income needs from the budget? If your net take-home pay is much larger than your target retirement income, then you need to address one of two questions: "What are you prepared to do without in retirement that you enjoy now?" or "Are you currently saving the difference between these two figures?"

It has been my experience that people generally tend to underestimate what they actually spend in any one area, unless they are keeping detailed records of their cash flow. Sometimes people get caught up in some of the general formulas that they hear, such as "You will need 70 per cent of your pre-retirement income when you retire." And while a generalization such as that may have some application during the accumulation years, it is far better for you to be more specific to your own situation as you approach retirement.

YOUR INCOME TARGET

(Monthly, after tax)

NEEDS		DISCRETIONARY	
Mortgage/Rent	_____	Vacations/Travel	_____
Property Taxes	_____	Restaurants	_____
Property Insurance	_____	Entertaining	_____
Water/Heat/Hydro	_____	Hobbies	_____
Condo Maintenance/Fees	_____	Gifts	_____
Property Maintenance	_____	Charitable Donations	_____
Food	_____	Memberships	_____
Clothing	_____	Recreational Property	_____
Instalment Loans	_____		
subtotal	_____	subtotal	_____

Life Insurance	_____		
Critical Illness Insurance	_____	Other	_____
Long-Term Care Insurance	_____	Other	_____
Health Insurance	_____	subtotal	_____
Dental Care	_____		
Prescription Drugs	_____		
Non-Prescription Drugs	_____		
Other Medical	_____		
subtotal	_____		

Auto Loan	_____
Auto Insurance	_____
Fuel	_____
Maintenance	_____
subtotal	_____

Other	_____
Other	_____
subtotal	_____

TOTAL NEEDS _____   **TOTAL DISCRETIONARY** _____

The other reason this exercise is so critical is that you then have to measure your income needs against the assets and sources of income you have available. You want to be comfortably confident that you have a sustainable level of withdrawal against your assets that will deliver this income well into your late eighties or early nineties. The questions you want to have answered are: "Will I have enough income to do the things I want to do" and "Do I have enough assets to make that income last?" If the projections in the blueprint show that income from personal assets will stop at age 81, the initial income needs you are looking at are too high in relation to the retirement assets you have. In that case, your alternatives are as follows:

- Move your retirement date further into the future—even two or three years can make a big difference.
- Scale down your income and lifestyle objectives in order to reduce the amount of income you need.
- Find some level of employment income to supplement what can be delivered from existing sources in order to meet your income target.

Allow me to say it once again: this is another reason why your blueprint is so important!

As I said in Chapter 1, retirement is not going to be a rewarding or fulfilling experience if you are constantly losing sleep over your finances. Retiring too early with too little is a decision that can fill you with regret.

The commencement of retirement involves charting some unknown waters. For all of the care put into planning, creating expectations and calculating income needs, there may end up being too much or too little income. Too much income is not tax effective and may hinder the battle against inflation. Too little income means that basic needs and wants are not being met. As a footnote to establishing an initial budget, it is important to also recognize that no matter how specific you try to be, statistically about half of those who are newly retired find that they end up spending more than they expected in their first two years of retirement.

And before you put that pay stub away . . .

In today's environment, the vast majority of people do not have the option to remain in group health and dental plans when they retire or exceed a certain age (65 or 70). The pay stub will show you what you are currently contributing for these benefits at work. Why not simply dovetail a similar allocation in retirement to fund individual health and dental programs? Your health and dental needs don't go away simply because you are retired. In fact, the opposite is true. Don't be without basic coverage!

Once you have arrived at that initial monthly after-tax number, you can look at the most efficient way to create it from the sources of income you have available. The plan should provide flexibility in its structure to allow for adjustments in the amount of income being delivered, depending on your changing needs throughout retirement.

Another Timing Scenario

There are times when people may have to approach retirement in a manner or on a basis of timing that is not ideal as it relates to the income they need and the assets they have. This is generally caused by unforeseen events over which they have little control, including:

- termination of existing employment (downsizing/layoff/plant closure)
- necessity to leave or change from current employment environment
- sudden and radical change of personal objectives
- sudden and radical change in the state of your health (or that of your spouse)

In this case, I reverse the process and determine what level of income can be provided and is sustainable from the various benefits and assets they have. This usually involves establishing a straight rate of withdrawal from assets in a way that will not erode the initial capital value. As suggested by the reasons listed above, the request for this type of calculation is usually the result of changes in Time Hub priorities. If this is the case, often the person will retire even if the actual numbers do not solidly support the move. And this, in turn, will mean adjusting their lifestyle to the income that can be generated or, if they are able, looking to some form of employment income to supplement cash flow.

Let me share with you the example of a situation where pension was triggered early to assist a client in transitioning from formal employment. When I first met Neil, he had been working for the same employer for 32 years. He was in the defined benefit pension plan for a national company and was finding, at age 56, that the strain of his job and of working shifts was becoming less tolerable as he was getting older. In addition to that, changes in management and corporate attitude meant that work "just wasn't fun anymore." That is a comment I hear frequently these days. He reached the point where he said that his being there was "carving years off of his life," and he just had to get out. So, we took a look at the details of his situation and here is what we discovered. He could not fully retire. There was a big difference between his employment income and the *pre-tax* income of his pension benefit. But, when we looked at the difference between the *after-tax* income he took home from his employment and the *after-tax* income that his pension would provide, the gap closed meaningfully. He did end up leaving his employer and starting his pension income, and now he works seasonally at something he really enjoys to make up the difference in cash flow that he requires. Last year, he started his CPP benefit, which, when added on an after-tax basis to his pension income, brings his income nearly to the amount he was bringing home prior to retiring. Now, I know that if he had stayed working rather than retiring early, he would have had a higher pension today. But since he left his long-term employer, he has been a very happy guy and has really enjoyed the transition. His health has improved and his blood pressure has slowly been returning to normal. There is a lot to be said for that, and it is something you cannot measure in monetary terms. This is also a classic case of transitioning, where someone is not fully employed and not fully retired, but a combination of both.

Spending Patterns and Dealing with Inflation

Okay, so you have determined the amount of initial monthly income you will require. But how will your income need to adjust over the years to maintain your purchasing power in the face of inflation? Inflation is an issue to people who are on fixed incomes. Even the current low levels of inflation we are experiencing will have a negative impact on your purchasing power over time. However, I have found that retirees do not require the same level of inflation-adjusted income all the way through their retirement. The reason for this is that there is a difference between life expectancy and years of good health. Let me be absolutely clear. You do need to plan for the effects of inflation and for potential health-related costs. The reality, however, is that people aged 84 don't spend money in the same way or on the same things as people aged 64. Spending tends to slow down as people age. All you have to do is look at your parents as an example of this. When my father was in his late eighties, he barely spent more than his monthly CPP and OAS payments. He didn't travel. Most of his monthly needs were met where he resided, and he really didn't have many other expenses.

Illustrations that show you requiring a fully-indexed income all the way through your retirement are basically wrong and are, in fact, misleading. Most retirees realize that the first 10 years of retirement, regardless of whether they retire at age 48 or 68, will be the best 10 years that they have. Statistically, using the averages in Canada, a male aged 65 can expect to live another 15 years, eight of which will be in good health. Females can expect to live another 19 years after age 65, nine of which will be free from major health problems. In the blueprints I prepare for my clients, I use the following model to project their ongoing income needs once I have established the initial cash flow they require. This allows me to address inflation concerns and also reflects the eventual reduction in spending patterns that consistently happens.

This projection of income needs takes the initial cash flow required and indexes it at an assumed rate of inflation. For the chart on the next page, we used an assumption of 2.5% per year. You can see that at age 75, I have shown a reduction in the amount of income that would be required (if I am working with a couple, I reduce income in the year where the younger person is age 75). I have shown a reduction of 25% in the graph. This is simply to reflect the reality, as previously stated, that people don't need a fully indexed level of income in retirement. I continue to show an inflation adjustment after the reduction at age 75 to maintain purchasing power and to address potential health-related costs that may increase.

FIGURE 3.2: Projected Cash Flow Needs

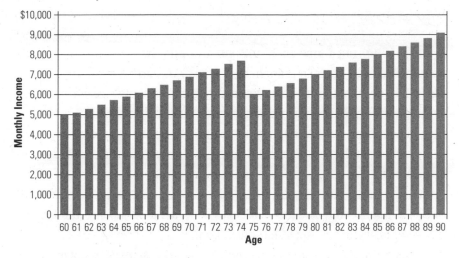

I have used this successfully for years. You may choose a different formula or method to reflect the points made above. From my experience, retirement income projections that do not adjust at all for inflation or that are fully indexed through retirement are both in error.

How Long Will You Need Your Income?

Obviously, "How long will you need your income?" is a question for which there is no precise answer, especially since life expectancy numbers continue to rise. You do not want to outlive your assets and income, but should you be running retirement income scenarios that assume you'll live to 110? Certain planners contend that income projections should extend until the younger of two married partners is 90. That is one option. Certainly, the average longevity numbers suggest that the majority of those about to retire today will make it into their eighties. Seeking a solution to this question is not part of an attempt to have your money deplete the month after you pass away. Again, it comes down to a practical application of using your assets in a way that provides both security and the option to do more things in the earlier, more vibrant years of retirement. Other considerations involve your spouse, if applicable. Will your spouse be retiring (or retired) at the same time as you? Is your spouse younger or older than you are? How would projections for his or her longevity compare in relation to yours? And that, in turn, brings us to planning issues regarding survivor income.

Income Planning Considerations for the Survivor

As it relates to a couple in retirement, it is very important that you and your advisor know what will change with respect to income streams or assets at the passing of either partner. It surprises me how often this area of planning is not addressed. And I have found this to be the case at nearly every stage of the retirement life cycle. These are the key questions that need to be addressed:

- What specific changes will occur to household income and benefits at the passing of either spouse?
- Are there any sources of income that will disappear immediately?
- Are there any sources of income that will disappear over time? If so, when? By how much?
- What level of income does that leave for the survivor?
- Is this amount of income sufficient to meet the survivor's objectives?
- Is asset ownership set up to allow simple and immediate transfer? Is this ownership appropriate given other estate plans?
- Do registered assets have appropriate beneficiary designations?
- Do RRIFs, LIFs or LRIFs provide for continued payments to the surviving spouse or lump-sum transfer?
- Are there any locked-in vehicles that can be unlocked upon transfer?
- Are all assets currently delivering income, or are there some that could be used later?
- Are there asset allocation changes to be made to the investments?
- What are the new beneficiary or estate arrangements that now need to be made to the income-producing assets?
- What will be the effect on the taxable income of the survivor now that income is only in the name of one person?

As obvious as this comment is, these questions need to be answered *before* something happens to one of the married partners. Don't roll your eyes at what you just read! I have had people come into my office for the first time, having just lost a spouse, and they had answers to few, if any, of the above questions. Do you and your spouse know the answers to what appears above? If not, you better make sure that you do.

At the time one of the married partners passes away, Time Hub and Money Hub priorities change. This is one of the major life-altering events. It also requires a review of overall planning and a redefinition of goals from this point forward. The blueprint will basically need to be redrafted for the survivor.

The Money Hub Priorities

At the start of this step in the Six-Step Plan, it was mentioned that the focus would be on creating the income you need and determining the assets that will be used to do so. The Money Hub worksheet helps your advisor to understand your priorities, values and views in relation to the use of your income-producing assets to create the cash flow you need. You can access it through the www.boomersblueprint.com website. Rank the following items in terms of importance to you, on a scale of 1 to 10, with 10 being extremely important. For the purposes of this book, I am putting only a short explanation after each consideration.

- Income security
  Are you concerned that you will outlive your income?

- Highest possible income today
  How important is it to you to trigger income from every source and asset that you have? The answer may depend on what resources you have and how much income is to be created. Does your state of health or that of your spouse suggest that there will be limited time to do the things you want to do?

- Coping with inflation
  This refers to having your income and assets grow in order to maintain your purchasing power.

- Tax reduction

    Is it important to you to explore strategies to pay less tax on
    your income? It may sound like a redundant question, but how
    important is this issue to you relative to the others listed here?

- Health-risk management

    How important is proper management of health care and long-
    term care to you? In addition, how significant are the issues
    surrounding how this care will be funded? Is it important that
    the use of your personal assets be minimized for this purpose?

- Using capital assets

    How important is it to you that the initial value of your income-
    producing assets stays intact? Is it a large concern if, in order
    to create the income needed, your asset balances decline over
    time?

- Wealth transfer

    How much of a priority is it to maximize the transfer of your
    estate assets to your heirs? How significant is it that planning be
    done so that more of your money goes to family rather than to
    the tax department?

Each of these items is important, but you need to know exactly how important they are to you relative to each other. For example, if the most
important thing to you is not running out of money, then "Income Security"
would be rated a 10. Then decide how the other considerations would rank
in relation to that. There are trade-offs in this process, and you need to
indicate your level of interest in or concern for each consideration. The
manner in which you rate these priorities will assist you and your advisor
in determining how and when different assets and benefits are used to create income. In addition, the answers you provide will give direction in the
areas of risk management and investment strategies.

Step 4. Layering Your Income

Now that you know what you want designed and why you want it, you can take the building materials available to you (your benefits and assets) and put together the blueprint. As has been mentioned, there are a lot of moving parts to this, and there is far more to this process than just the investment portfolio.

Determining the amount of income to be delivered and the most efficient way to deliver it should really be done on a year-by-year basis. There are many changes that people experience as they go through the various stages of their retirement. Their income objectives and needs will also change.

Part Three looks at the different forms of income available to you in the order that I believe they should be used. As you read through the points on layering, you will see the rationale behind the way these sources of income were listed. Layering involves creating the income you need from the assets and sources you have available. It incorporates a number of concepts and ultimately combines the following actions:

1. Using the least flexible income sources as they are available

    Obviously, you have no control over the amount of income that comes from government benefits or pension income in the form of an annuity. While they are guaranteed sources, they are also inflexible. They should form the base of your income and you should leave your more flexible personal assets to layer income on top of these.

2. Using the least tax-efficient income sources in lower tax brackets

    These, conveniently, are for the most part the same sources of income mentioned in the above point. CPP, OAS, pension income, interest from non-registered assets, LIF, LRIF, RLIF and RRIF payments are among those which are fully taxable. As your level of taxable income increases, you eventually move into higher tax brackets. As such, it makes sense to use these sources of income first so that they are being taxed at lower rates.

3. Working efficiently within the tax brackets

   Although this does tie in with the next action, it also involves
   strategically unravelling fully-taxable assets such as RRSPs and
   RRIFs and converting them to non-registered holdings. This
   "topping up to bracket" strategy is covered in Part Three.

4. Putting the least amount of "strain" on an asset to deliver the next
   dollar to spend

   This is complementary to the first two actions. As your taxable
   income moves into higher tax brackets, it is far more efficient to
   create the cash flow you need from tax-favoured or non-taxable
   sources. You want to use the more tax-efficient layers at higher
   marginal rates and the least tax-efficient ones at lower tax rates.
   This would require a smaller amount of withdrawal from an
   asset to provide an after-tax dollar, compared to a source of
   income that is fully taxable. This may sound like a fairly obvious
   and logical course of action, but so often I meet people who are
   using tax-efficient assets in lower tax brackets and fully-taxable
   sources of income in higher brackets. This is just so inefficient
   and totally contrary to preserving your income-producing assets.

5. Looking for income-splitting and asset-splitting opportunities

   This is all in an attempt to keep your net income figure relatively
   low. That, in turn, allows you to preserve as many government
   benefits as possible. You will likely lose some of them due to
   your level of net income. The point is not to lose them needlessly, now or in the future.

6. Determining which personal assets are best to use to create income
   and which are best to defer

   This is so important and an area of planning where I find great
   misunderstanding and inefficiencies. It will be examined in
   much more detail in Chapter 8, which focuses on taxation.
   Traditional thinking would suggest you defer all of your registered assets and use your non-registered investments first when

creating income. Yet for the majority of retirees, the reverse works more effectively over time.

Layering is income planning in the most specific sense. It is the year-by-year determination of how to create the income that you need from the sources available to you, in the most efficient way.

MAKING YOUR BLUEPRINT WORK FOR YOU

1. The first step of the Six-Step Plan is to assess where you are in terms of your life stage in retirement.

2. For Step 2, think through some of the lifestyle and Time Hub considerations so that you have an idea of how you will be spending your time and how much income you'll need to do so.

3. In Step 3, determine the initial level of retirement income that you'll require and distinguish between wants and needs and give some thought to continuing to provide an income to a surviving spouse.

4. Step 4 involves layering your incomes in an efficient way so that you spend the least flexible and least tax-efficient ones first.

4

PUTTING YOUR MONEY TO WORK

Step 5. Aligning Your Investments with Your Income Plan

Your investments are *not* your retirement blueprint. They are the tools and solutions you'll need to execute your blueprint once it has been drafted. They are important, but they need to be set up in conjunction with strategies that are appropriate and proven in a withdrawal scenario and should complement the blueprint. I watch business and investment programs on TV and lament the fact that what is pushed at people non-stop is that investment selection is key. That is not true. Your blueprint is your guiding influence. The investments must address your plan, not the other way around. As stated very early in this book, this time in your financial life should be planning and process driven, not product driven.

As such, I am approaching this section from the point of view of strategy rather than trying to suggest to you that one particular financial product works better than another. You and/or your advisor may prefer to use mutual funds, ETFs, individual stocks and bonds, managed fund portfolios, segregated funds, variable annuities or any combination of these. I am not going to go through the potential investment options one by one and compare features. That is for you and your advisor to work through. What I am going to do is focus on those things that I have found to really make a difference in planning and investing within a withdrawal scenario. This includes appropriate asset mix, otherwise known as asset allocation, and

investment strategies that I have found to work effectively to create retirement income.

The Balancing Act

During your accumulation years, the emphasis is on saving money and building assets. Often people will measure the effectiveness of or value provided
by their advisor by the investment returns that they experience. However,
when people begin to draw income from their portfolios, their focus changes
from "rate of return" to "risk management." Capital preservation becomes
the number one issue, because with capital preservation, you also have sustainable income. Yes, returns are still important, but the primary objective is
to make sure that the income-producing assets have *longevity*.

FIGURE 4.1: Saving Years Versus Retirement Years

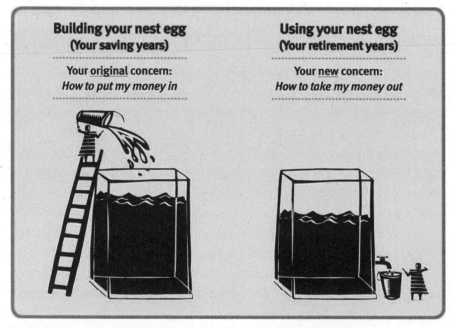

Reprinted with permission of RBC Financial: Your Future By Design—Your Lifestyle Choices

The graphic above can be viewed in two very different ways. At a pre-
retirement workshop, attendees were asked to express how they would feel
if this represented their first year of retirement. They started with the nest

egg at a level shown in the bucket on the left. At the end of year one, the
account value had shrunk by meaningfully more than the total withdrawn
for income, to the level shown in the bucket on the right. If that were the
case, how would they react? Would they stick with their plan? Would they
panic? Would they reduce the amount of withdrawal they were making?

As discussion was ending, one of the attendees asked a great question
that represented another valid way of looking at this situation. He asked,
"How would you feel if that was how things looked at the end of year
thirty-one rather than year one? You still have nearly all of your money, but
you haven't done any of the things you were really hoping to do in retirement." And that prompted an interesting discussion. Almost every person
felt that the money that had been saved during the accumulation years
should be used to make retirement a fulfilling experience. In the income
years, there is a need to balance both the short-term and long-term use of
assets. It is true that retirees do not want to run out of money. But neither
do they want to be idle in their retirement years and pass away with vast
amounts of unused wealth.

Establishing investment portfolios for a withdrawal scenario is an
interesting challenge for advisors, as clients have a very different set of
demands and expectations compared to the accumulation years. As their
advisors, clients expect us:

- to *preserve* assets by managing risk while helping them *use* their
  assets to fund their retirement lifestyle
- to invest conservatively, yet have some growth in their assets to
  deal with future inflation issues
- to be instrumental in planning and facilitating the transfer of
  wealth to survivors, heirs or estate; part of this process involves
  some of the other risk considerations, such as potential health-risk
  costs
- revise and revisit these considerations through different life stages

Some of the objectives may seem to be opposed to one another, yet these
all must be addressed by investors and advisors at the time retirement
income is being created. Keep in mind, as well, that your priorities and

objectives will change over time. For the advisor, it is somewhat like trying to put together a jigsaw puzzle while the picture on the box keeps changing. It is indeed a balancing act.

It is also essential to realize some other very important realities. There are things over which you and your advisor can have some control and influence and many things over which you have no control whatsoever.

What You Cannot Control	What You Can Control
Stock markets	Your asset allocation
Interest rates	Which investments will create income
Inflation	Investment costs
Currency	Navigating the tax brackets
Other people's behaviour	Which assets you use and which you defer

So why would you or your advisor worry about or waste time on the things you can't control? The focus should be on those issues and aspects of your investment portfolio that you can influence.

Withdrawal Models

There are a great many models and theories to examine when trying to determine an appropriate level of withdrawal from income-producing assets. The main challenge is not only to sustain purchasing power but also to preserve the assets generating the income so as not to outlive your money. Some samples of withdrawal models include the following.

The 4 per cent rule

Based on his early research of actual stock market returns and retirement scenarios over the past 75 years, William Bengen found that retirees who draw down no more than 4.2 per cent of their portfolio in the initial year and adjust that amount every year thereafter for inflation stand a greater chance that their money will outlive them. His analysis also showed that retirees who draw down at a rate of 5 per cent a year (again, adjusted annually for inflation) run a 30 per cent chance of exhausting their income-producing assets.

This model assumes that retirees need a fully-indexed level of income all the way through their retirement, and I have found that this is inaccurate.

An additional complication in looking at U.S. models is the inclusion of health-care costs. I want to emphasize that we *do* have health care–related costs in Canada, but not to the same degree as in the United States.

Risk-adjusted total return

This model focuses on building well-diversified portfolios based on client-specific risk parameters. The process is to draw down on these accounts at a withdrawal rate of between 3 and 6 per cent. At that level of withdrawal, it is anticipated that income can be sustained. Your income-producing assets will have years when the investment returns are in excess of the amount of withdrawals and your assets grow in value. There will also be years when returns are lower than the amount of withdrawal, or even negative, and this will serve to reduce the value of your income-producing assets. But by monitoring the rate of withdrawal to a generally accepted rate, the expectation is that income can be sustained even though account values will fluctuate.

Duration-based portfolios

This model is based on the concept of "bucketing" or "separate buckets." This simply involves separating income-producing assets into three different "buckets," which are intended to be used over short-, medium- and long-term time horizons. Each bucket then has its own appropriate investment strategy.

Short-term needs – protection and guarantees
Intermediate needs – conservatively balanced investments
Long-term needs – growth-oriented investments

Income allocation

This approach advocates the combination of defined income streams, such as CPP, OAS and pensions from employment, with guaranteed annuities, variable annuities and withdrawals from variable investment portfolios. This provides a combination of certainty and flexibility. The refined version of this strategy as promoted by the Retirement Income Industry Association (RIIA) is to take a "Floor and Upside" approach. This involves creating a "floor" of guaranteed income that the client(s) cannot outlive to fund what are defined as cash flow *needs*. Once that is established, the balance of the income-producing assets are invested to generate income for *discretionary* items and provide an opportunity for asset growth. The charts below illustrate the two steps in this process.

Step One: Ensure that income for basic needs is created through guarantees

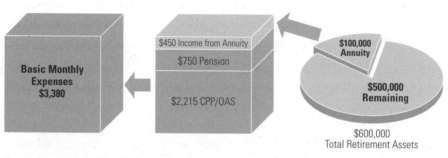

Household needs and income shown on a before-tax basis.

So, in this example, $3,380 of pre-tax cash flow was required to fund the needs of the household. Between the CPP/OAS entitlement and a smaller pension payment, the guaranteed household income was $2,965 monthly. But the needs required cash flow of $3,380. So the guaranteed floor was created by taking $100,000 from the accumulated assets and acquiring a variable annuity that, at a 5 per cent payout, creates income of $415 monthly. So for now, the essential expenses are covered by guaranteed income.

Step Two: Pay for discretionary expenses with remainder of your portfolio

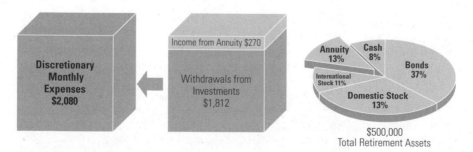

Household needs and income shown on a before-tax basis. Assumes $65,000 dedicated to annuity with remaining $435,000 providing income stream equal to a 5% withdrawal.

The discretionary expense items required an additional $2,080 of cash flow. This amount can be drawn from the $500,000 that remains after the purchase of the variable annuity in Step One.

So the required total cash flow is $5,460 per month, with the necessary expenses being fully covered by guaranteed sources of income. Regardless of market performance or interest rates, the essential expenses are certain to be addressed. That is the floor and upside approach.

You should also consider what the impact would be on both the expenses and the cash flow needed should one of the two partners in this example pass away. For example, one OAS payment would stop and CPP income would be reduced to a survivor benefit. If that occurred in 2011, the total CPP/OAS would be $1,496 for the survivor, compared to the current $2,215. So a reassessment of the needs of the survivor would be necessary. Once that new number is established, you must make sure it is covered by the existing guaranteed income and add new guaranteed sources if needed.

In my practice, I have used all of these different approaches. On occasion I have even combined them in order to best address client needs, priorities and preferences. As part of the risk-adjusted total return approach, I employ an income process called the Cash Wedge, which will be described in more detail in a few pages.

Risk Management: Protecting Your Income-Producing Assets

In the retirement income market, capital preservation is critical. That is one reason why ensuring that you have a realistic, sustainable withdrawal rate is so key. Traditionally, clients think of investment risk as the *only* danger to their income-producing assets. In fact, there are many risks that can erode the income-generating assets over time. They include longevity risk, encroachment risk, taxation risk, inflation risk, health-cost risk and withdrawal risk.

Longevity risk

This simply means running out of money before you run out of time. It is one of the greatest financial fears for retirees. There have been numerous articles on this topic, spawned by the market debacle of 2008 and 2009. I have a friend and client who is a doctor by profession. She once commented, "It is frustrating to hear about the health care 'crisis' in Canada. We don't have people dying in the streets because they can't get attention. People aren't being refused treatment. Yes, there are some challenges, but I get tired of hearing about this 'crisis.' It is not an accurate assessment." Likewise, for retirees, there are challenges when stock markets fall 33 per cent and interest rates are at 50-year lows. It is very easy for people, especially those in retirement, to become very anxious about their situation. But really, you can't outlive CPP and OAS, and as you get older, you can acquire a life annuity on a very favourable basis. There may have to be some adjustments in lifestyle or tough decisions made in the absolute worst case scenario. But, if you have government benefits and personal assets, it is not a question of completely running out of income.

Encroachment risk

Encroachment risk occurs when the amount of regular withdrawals exceeds the rate of growth in the account, thereby reducing the principal. This can result in a gradual depletion of the income-producing assets. It is like many of the slot machines in a casino (so I've heard), where you put your money in but don't win or lose on one spin. That would frustrate the gamblers, because they obviously would end up losing far more times than they would win. So the machine lets them "win" many times while they play, but in most cases what they win is less than what they bet. So their stake dwindles even though they get the sense that they are doing just fine (again, so I've heard). Okay, so here we go from a retirement income perspective. If you are trying to be cautious and have everything in GICs or bonds at the interest rates prevailing at the start of 2011, your overall portfolio may be producing a 3 per cent return. If you are withdrawing 5 per cent, you are gradually going to erode the value of your account. You actually put your assets at risk by trying to be too conservative. By the way, I am *not* equating investing to gambling. I am simply stating an obvious point that sometimes gets missed. Accounts can be depleted even when returns are positive—if the withdrawals are happening at a greater rate than those returns.

TABLE 4.4: The Impact of Encroachment Risk

Assumptions: $500,000 capital, income withdrawal of $25,000 (5%) annually

		Return				
		Full 5%	4.50%	4.00%	3.50%	2.50%
Years	5	$500,000	$480,169	$467,502	$455,089	$431,011
	10	$500,000	$455,455	$427,963	$401,750	$352,956
	15	$500,000	$424,658	$379,858	$338,399	$264,643
	20	$500,000	$386,279	$321,332	$263,158	$164,762
	25	$500,000	$338,451	$250,125	$173,795	$ 51,679

Even a small difference in investment return, relative to your withdrawal rate, can make a big difference over time. There is a real danger in being too conservative in times when guaranteed rates are at 50-year lows.

Taxation risk

Higher rates of taxation can put unnecessary strain on assets to produce the after-tax income required. This is detailed in Part Four. Higher levels of net income may also reduce or eliminate government benefits and tax credits. So although, on the surface, this may not appear to be much of a risk, any time there are additional withdrawals required from your income-producing assets to produce the same after-tax income, that represents a risk to preserving those assets.

Inflation risk

Assets need to be invested in such a manner that there is some potential for growth in addition to income. Increases in income will be required over time simply to maintain purchasing power in the face of inflation. Experience has shown repeatedly that retirees do not need a fully inflation-adjusted income all the way through retirement. There does, however, need to be some growth in the assets to enable them to deliver an increase in income while keeping the withdrawal rate the same.

Health-cost risk

Income-producing assets may be reduced or depleted if accessed to cover health-related costs. Not everything is paid for by provincial health care, and coverage varies greatly from province to province. This could be something as minor as increasing prescription drug costs or as major as funding the long-term care required by a spouse.

Withdrawal risk

This refers to the danger of making withdrawals in years where investment returns are negative. It is also referred to as "sequential risk." Below I use three tables to illustrate this.

Variable Investment Math

Compound Rates of Return, Annual Returns

Year	1	2	3	4	5	6	7	8	9	10	Return
(A)	7	7	7	7	7	7	7	7	7	7	7%
(B)	9.9	14	13	23	-4	10	-1	21	-4	-7	7%
(C)	-7	-4	21	-1	10	-4	23	13	14	9.9	7%

If you had an investment that returned 7 per cent per year over a 10-year period, you would end up with a compound (or annualized) rate of return of 7 per cent. That is shown in result (A). But the investment returns in variable portfolios don't fall out in this linear fashion. So I found a Canadian balanced mutual fund that had a return of 7 per cent compound over a 10-year period. Result (B) shows how the returns actually occurred for that fund for each year over that 10-year period. To continue this exercise, I then took that order of actual returns and reversed them, giving result (C). Now we have a situation where the initial returns were negative, but the end result after 10 years was unchanged at 7 per cent. So what we have are three different investment scenarios all resulting in an annualized 10-year rate of return of 7 per cent.

Accumulation Math

$100,000 Deposit: Invested for 10 Years, No Withdrawals, Annual Returns

Year	1	2	3	4	5	6	7	8	9	10	End Value
(A)	7	7	7	7	7	7	7	7	7	7	$196,715
(B)	9.9	14	13	23	-4	10	-1	21	-4	-7	$196,715
(C)	-7	-4	21	-1	10	-4	23	13	14	9.9	$196,715

Now let's look at what happens when you are accumulating assets. Assume you had $100,000 to invest and received the same investment experience and returns as in the first scenario. Irrespective of how the returns are realized, there is no effect on either the annualized return or the accumulation balance. That is a basic rule of mathematics. In multiplication, the order of factors does not affect the resulting product.

Withdrawal Math
$100,000 Deposit: $7,000 Planned Annual Withdrawal, Annual Returns

Year	1	2	3	4	5	6	7	8	9	10	End Value
(A)	7	7	7	7	7	7	7	7	7	7	$100,000
(B)	9.9	14	13	23	-4	10	-1	21	-4	-7	$112,528
(C)	-7	-4	21	-1	10	-4	23	13	14	9.9	$ 83,586

However, when you are drawing income from your portfolio, the order of investment returns has a significant impact on your assets. As you can see in scenario (C), when withdrawals are being made and you have negative investment returns in the early years, there is a very negative impact on the value of the income-producing asset. What you basically have when you are drawing out income and you experience negative investment returns is a "double drawdown" effect. This is further emphasized when comparing the difference in account values, at the end of 10 years, between results (C) and (B). It is $28,942, or 35 per cent. Often people (and planning illustration software) assume that if a portfolio averages a rate of return of 7 per cent, a withdrawal rate of the same amount should leave the capital intact. That would be true in result (A) and if the returns were credited to the account at the same time the withdrawal was being made. In reality, variable returns never fall out in a straight line and can have a significant impact—both positive and negative—on the income scenario and on the asset value of your portfolio.

In as much as this is a valid concern and it does pose a risk, the degree of risk is also largely influenced by the withdrawal rate that is being used. That is one key factor to risk management in a withdrawal scenario. Another is having proper diversity and balance within your investment portfolio. The use of an appropriate withdrawal rate in the range of 5 to 6 per cent along with a withdrawal process, such as the Cash Wedge strategy, goes a long way to preserving income-producing assets.

The Cash Wedge: An Income Delivery Process

The "Cash Wedge" is what I call the income delivery process I developed in 1993 and have been using successfully ever since. It helps to address the issues that you cannot control by allowing you to focus on those aspects over which you do have some influence.

FIGURE 4.5: The Cash Wedge

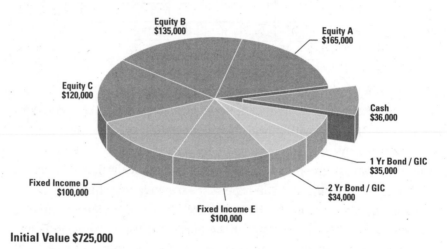

Equity B
$135,000

Equity A
$165,000

Equity C
$120,000

Cash
$36,000

1 Yr Bond / GIC
$35,000

2 Yr Bond / GIC
$34,000

Fixed Income D
$100,000

Fixed Income E
$100,000

Initial Value $725,000

The process

The Cash Wedge is a withdrawal model that incorporates a number of income and investment concepts within it, some of which have already been discussed. It is used for both registered and non-registered investments. And although it is not complicated, it does require review and it does require maintenance. The periodic rebalancing makes beneficial use of the variance in performance between asset classes. Here are the steps that make it function effectively.

1. The first thing that needs to be established is the asset allocation (equity-to-fixed-income mix) that is appropriate for you. That is a

discussion for you and your advisor. You can also find online questionnaires that will help you determine what the most appropriate asset mix is, given your objectives, tolerances and timeline. In the figure above, I have shown a 60 per cent equity, 40 per cent fixed-income allocation. For this explanation, let's assume this is your account.

2. Within the fixed-income portion of the portfolio, create a cash position equal to the income needed for the first 12 months. You will draw your income from this cash position. This is the source for your income because cash does not fluctuate. Also acquire a one-year and a two-year GIC or bond in order to create the source of income for years two and three. As they mature, simply move the proceeds to the cash account to replenish it and continue your income withdrawals. At the outset, this provides three years of guaranteed income. It could also be set up for two or four years, depending on your situation and your preferences. On this portfolio size, an annual withdrawal rate of about 5 per cent provides withdrawals of $3,000 per month, or $36,000 for the year.

3. The initial cash amount of $36,000 and the GICs/bonds are part of the 40 per cent of the portfolio allocated to a fixed-income mandate. The two other fixed-income segments in the pie chart round out the 40 per cent. The 60 per cent equity component is shown as three separate positions, which could be Canadian equity, U.S. equity and international equity. You still want to have some diversification within specific asset classes.

4. If the equity selections provide investment returns that will allow you to take profits and replenish the Cash Wedge, it may make sense to renew the GICs or bonds. The objective is to maintain a multiple of income payments within the Cash Wedge by taking profits where and when appropriate from the other investments within the portfolio. You want to maintain it but not have too much money in this form.

5. Any profits realized that do not need to be used to restore the Cash
   Wedge can be used to acquire additional units or positions in the investments that are flat or negative. If you have proper diversification
   in your investments, you should expect to have one or more of your
   asset classes/investments in a flat or negative position when your
   account is being reviewed. They should not all be performing in
   the same way at the same time. This is a sell-high, buy-low process
   that will likely result in higher returns over time. In addition, it will
   allow the portfolio to experience a lower degree of volatility. I'm not
   suggesting that you simply divest of good investments, but that you
   have a process through which you take profits and maintain them. It
   is important to note that all of this is done with an eye to maintaining the appropriate asset mix that was established at the outset.

6. This process also affords you the opportunity to be selective in terms
   of which specific investments you use to create income. These are
   all planning efficiencies that I will address and that you will see listed in the "Investment Considerations for Your Withdrawal Portfolio"
   section.

Notes on the Cash Wedge

I have deliberately used the terms "equity, fixed income and cash" in the
investment descriptions. So whether this is being set up with individual
securities, mutual funds, segregated funds, ETFs or whatever, that's between you and your advisor. It is the mechanics of the process that are key
to making it work.

When I meet with people for the first time, I will ask them if they can
explain the investment strategy that has been put in place for them by their
existing advisor or institution. In the vast majority of cases, they cannot
describe it. Whether they can or they can't, next to no one has ever been
able to answer the follow-up question, which is: "What is the income strategy that has been put in place in order for your investments to produce the
cash flow you will need?" Normally they just look at me when I ask that
question, go quiet and tilt their head to one side. It sort of looks like the
pose of the dog on the label of RCA-Victor records. As I have said several

times, the strategy for the withdrawal years will be very different from the one for the accumulation years.

Lastly, this process obviously does not prevent markets from declining, nor does it negate the reality that your portfolio assets will definitely decline in those times when markets do fall. However, it will reduce the necessity of having to collapse investments that are down in value in order to deliver income and, more importantly, it allows those investments that have fallen the opportunity to heal over time. Today, two years after the market lows of March 2009, basically all of the investment values in my clients' accounts have been restored. That was able to happen because there was a process in place that could strategically deliver the income needed while allowing some time for the equity markets to recover.

Additional Investment Considerations for Your Withdrawal Portfolio

There are a number of strategies and considerations that will be beneficial to you in obtaining the maximum benefit from your income-producing assets. Some of these have already been addressed, such as:

- consolidate assets
- consider income streams as well as assets
- layer income in a specific order
- provide the potential for some growth
- adopt a model for income delivery

In addition to the above points, the following will also assist you to improve the efficiency with which your income is being created, reduce taxation and preserve your income-producing assets. Some of these actions are straightforward, simple and obvious, and yet I see many situations where they are still not being done properly. All of these resulting improvements will help sustain your retirement income.

Allocate for tax efficiency

This is so basic that I am almost embarrassed to write it down. Have your tax-inefficient investments within registered accounts or other shelters, such as a TFSA or corporate class mutual fund. If you are going to have interest-bearing investments, hold them in an account that is sheltered. As I describe in Part Three, there are tools that you can use to be more efficient when setting up your mix of equity and fixed income in both registered and non-registered accounts. Think "overall" asset mix vs. "by account" asset mix. But for heaven's sake, there are ways to put this together within your risk profile and not lose so much of your currently pitiful fixed-income returns to taxation. There, I said it . . . but I'm still blushing.

Follow an investment and income process

Ideally, the process and the strategy for managing the assets and creating the income streams should be documented through an instrument known as an Investment Policy Statement (IPS). It is written with input from you and your advisor, and it provides understanding and direction to the entire investment process. It also serves to create a more systematic and disciplined approach to ongoing decision-making. The use of an IPS in conjunction with a detailed, written financial plan enhances the potential success in meeting investment objectives. Just as important, it plays a significant role in limiting investor mistakes and in quantifying expectations. Your IPS should include the following:

- review of your objectives, circumstances and investment tolerances
- specifics of the asset mix and target rate of return
- details of the asset allocation mix and specific investments
- guidelines for portfolio/manager evaluation
- triggers for action, including rebalancing, taking profits and replacing managers
- disclosure of the fees associated with the investments chosen
- expectations/commitments for service

It should serve as a communication tool between you and your advisor, and along with your blueprint, it should be the basis for discussion at review meetings. A very good friend of mine says, "When it comes to any business dealings, good paper makes good friends." It is true here, as well.

Be selective

Whether you are stripping profits or drawing directly from an investment, you do not want to be drawing down on any holdings that have fallen in value. Be selective in terms of which investments are to be used to create your income payments. Much use is made of balanced funds and structured portfolios during the accumulation years. However, at the time you are creating income, these vehicles are not as efficient, unless you are dealing with a smaller account size. For example, you cannot direct the fund company to pay the income needed out of the bond portion of a balanced fund. Generating income from it will simply involve a surrender of units, which in turn reflects the proportionate composition of that fund or portfolio. Separate investments, funds or pools are a preferable structure so that the specific source of withdrawals can be more clinically determined. That is one of the reasons why the Cash Wedge strategy is so effective.

Think of it in these terms: When I was a kid, we would get the big bucket of Neapolitan ice cream from the dairy. Ah yes, chocolate, strawberry and vanilla, all there to enjoy. But our dairy in those days swirled the flavours so that they were blended together. I was not a big fan of the vanilla, but I loved the chocolate and strawberry. So, with the hands of a surgeon, I would carve around the vanilla marbling strips to get the other ice cream flavours I wanted. If you just took a scoop out, you got all three. That is like a withdrawal from a balanced fund or portfolio. What I am advocating by being specific in your withdrawals is like having individual buckets of vanilla, chocolate and strawberry ice cream—you can get 100 per cent of what you want.

This is one of the reasons why you need to exercise some caution with what are commonly known as Systematic Withdrawal Plans (SWPs). This is where you withdraw a certain dollar amount from a mutual fund on a scheduled basis. You don't want to be doing this, of course, from any positions that are down in value. That is why the Cash Wedge strategy has such merit.

Seek lower volatility

Another difference between the accumulation years and withdrawal years is how the level of volatility affects an investment portfolio. Here is a very simplistic example to make the point.

Figure 4.6 shows three different market conditions over a 10-year period:

1. a constantly increasing unit or share value, growing from $5.00 to $10.00
2. the same overall growth in unit value during the same time frame, but with greater fluctuation in unit value each year
3. a sharp initial decline followed by a recovery, so that after 10 years we have returned to the same starting unit or share value of $5.00

FIGURE 4.6: $1,200 Program Under Three Different Conditions Over a 10-Year Period

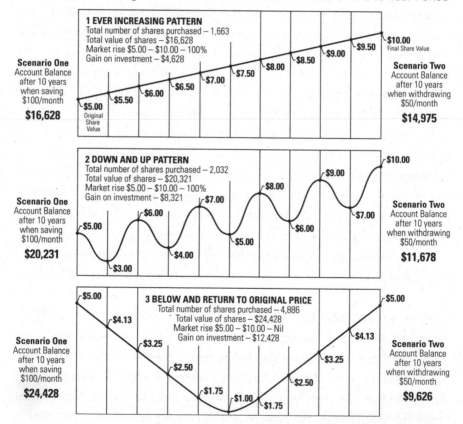

Let's take those market conditions and apply two different scenarios.

Scenario One is for the accumulation years. In fact, the accompanying chart is often used to illustrate the benefits of dollar-cost averaging.

The message here is that what people normally want (values that increase steadily), which is shown on the first graph, is not what will provide the best returns for them if they are making regular contributions. The market conditions clients usually don't want are the ones that will actually generate higher returns when they are putting money in. Stated another way, higher volatility is good for your account if you are making regular contributions. In Figure 4.6, the account balance is highest at $24,428 for the investment experience with the greatest volatility. That is what is referred to as the benefit of dollar-cost averaging in a fluctuating market.

Scenario Two, using the same market conditions, looks at a situation where we start with $12,000 and withdraw $50 per month over the 10-year time frame. Here the results are exactly contrary to what was experienced through dollar-cost averaging over the 10 years of accumulation. The more boring, straight-up market was best for a withdrawal scenario.

We are back to that "balancing act" once again. Income portfolios still need some potential for growth, but under conditions where volatility is reduced. Dollar-cost averaging in reverse can be harmful to the portfolio generating income. In a withdrawal environment, the lower the volatility within a variable portfolio, the better the end result. We can't control the volatility of the market, but even within equity positions there are more conservative options such as dividend-paying stocks. This is also why the Cash Wedge is such a valuable strategy to implement. Aside from allowing you to be very specific in terms of which investments you use for withdrawals, it also serves to moderate the overall volatility of your portfolio. Both of those features can assist in preserving your income-producing assets.

Look for a reasonable fee structure

The table below shows different asset combinations and the potential average yields that could be generated before fees. It then shows what the actual investor return or yield would be given different fee levels. Obviously, the higher the fees for given return, the lower the yield to you. Not as obvious is the fact that the vast majority of investors don't know how this impacts them because most don't know the level of fees they are paying for their investments.

TABLE 4.7: The Yield Challenge

Assumptions: (Pre-fee) annual returns of Equity, 10% and Bond, 5%
Simplified Example: $100,000 capital

		Net Returns to Investor				
		1.5%	2.0%	2.5%	3.0%	3.5%
Asset Mix	**Income**					
40% Equity	$4,000					
60% Bonds	$3,000					
Yield	**7.0%**	5.5%	5.0%	4.5%	4.0%	3.5%
50% Equity	$5,000					
50% Bonds	$2,500					
Yield	**7.5%**	6.0%	5.5%	5.0%	4.5%	4.0%
60% Equity	$6,000					
40% Bonds	$2,000					
Yield	**8.0%**	6.5%	6.0%	5.5%	5.0%	4.5%
80% Equity	$8,000					
20% Bonds	$1,000					
Yield	**9.0%**	7.5%	7.0%	6.5%	6.0%	5.5%

Basically, all variable investment products have a management fee. It is how revenues are generated in the investment industry. This fee is a cost you pay for the investment and, potentially, for other services, including, in most cases, advisor compensation. Often this fee is not transparent, in that you do not see it deducted from your gross returns. It is common for an investor to see only their net returns after fees have already been deducted. This is totally in line with the manner in which the securities regulators require they be quoted. I use the word "pay" because, although you likely don't write a cheque, these fees are deducted from your account and your returns.

The range of fees on variable investments can run anywhere from about 0.25 per cent per annum to nearly 4 per cent per annum, depending on the investment option and advisor compensation. As stated above, these amounts are deducted from your overall returns.

One of the components in the fee structure is what is referred to as "imbedded compensation." This is an amount paid to your advisor or the institution with whom you work. As a consumer what you need to know is:

- What is the total management expense ratio I am paying?
- What amount of the fee is for additional benefits or features of this investment?
- How much of this fee is for service and advice?
- What am I receiving from my advisor or institution for the fee I am paying?

The cost-to-benefit relationship relative to fees and advice/service is more transparent if your institution or advisor is actually adding a fee to an investment option where compensation is not imbedded. This is the usual practice where ETFs, pools or F-series mutual funds are used as the investment options.

Fees are a fact of investing. But you should be able to answer the four questions listed above, and the fees charged to you, in whatever manner they are charged, should be reasonable for what you are receiving in exchange for them.

Engage a sustainable withdrawal rate

What is an appropriate level for withdrawal from a variable portfolio in order to sustain the income being drawn over the long term? RIIA research has suggested the following in terms of withdrawal rates in relation to asset value:

Excess funding = <3.6 per cent
Constrained = >3.5 per cent < 7.1 per cent
Underfunded = > 7 per cent

This means that if the total withdrawals from your income-producing assets are less than 3.6 per cent, you actually have a situation where you have more assets than you need to create the income you desire. If you are drawing at a rate in excess of 7 per cent, then you are likely to find yourself in a situation where you are eroding your income-producing assets and eventually both the asset and the income being drawn from it will exhaust.

The range of 3.5 to 7.0 per cent is shown as "constrained," which simply means that while it is very practical to have sustainable income at that rate of withdrawal, some vigilance is required. I have preferred using a withdrawal rate of around 5 per cent, indexed, which has proven to be quite resilient in the face of negative markets over the last 20 years. Tables showing the effect and impact of a 5 per cent withdrawal rate follow later in this chapter. I have gone up to 6 per cent with some clients, but only in certain circumstances.

It is appropriate to have a sustainable withdrawal rate in mind as you are taking your income. It can even serve as a guide to tell you if you have enough money to retire. If you are retired, it can provide some insight as to whether or not your investments will be able to sustain themselves at your current level of withdrawals. There are additional considerations regarding withdrawal rates and withdrawal models, including the ones below.

- Everyone's situation is unique. There are no cookie-cutter solutions.
- Upon investigation, you will have a bias and/or preference for or against various solutions.
- Advisors will have a preferred solution approach and bias.
- It is an ever-evolving scenario that requires ongoing discussion and revision.
- Problems also arise when mathematical theory confronts reality. That does not make having a model for withdrawal useless. It does, however, suggest that there needs to be a balance between certainty and flexibility. Some of the variables that complicate withdrawal plans include the following:
  - changes in health
  - death
  - change in marital status
  - taxation considerations
  - conflicting client objectives
  - changing client objectives
  - the annual "once in a lifetime" financial crisis that people often have

This is also why, when people are deciding if they can retire, it is not necessarily as simple as saying that you need to have a million dollars. Different retirement lifestyles are going to require different levels of income and different rates of withdrawal. So a million dollars as a benchmark may be just right, not enough or far more than is necessary, depending on what the required withdrawals will be. That again is why determining lifestyle needs is the second step in this process.

Sustainable withdrawal rate and variable investment math

A few pages ago we looked at three examples to show how your investment portfolio can be negatively impacted over a 10-year period if you are withdrawing income when markets decline. The example was for the 10-year period ending in 2001 because these tables were used in my book *Buying Time*, which was released at the start of 2002. That is also why I was using 7 per cent as a return and withdrawal rate; the number seemed reasonable at the time. The following tables take the same information from that "withdrawal mathematics" example.

In each of the tables that follow, the first two columns show the year and the amount of annual income to be paid out. Column (B) Returns shows the actual, annual return history of the balanced fund from 1992 to the end of 2001. The resulting year-end account value after withdrawals is shown in (B) Account Value. (C) Returns reverses the order in which the returns were realized from 1992 to 2001, so that the negative returns occurred in the early years. And (C) Account Value shows the year-end balance after withdrawals have been made. That 10-year period takes us to the end of 2001. But what does this look like if we extend this history, given the market disaster of 2008 and the start of 2009? From 2002 to the end of 2010, both (B) Returns and (C) Returns show the same investment experience. I am just extending the scenario from the end of 2001 to show how the returns from the first 10 years have a long-term impact going forward. Four tables illustrate different withdrawal scenarios, all starting from an account balance of $100,000.

TABLE 4.8: 7% Withdrawal

Year	Income	(B) Returns	(B) Account Value	(C) Returns	(C) Account Value
1992	$7,000	9.90%	$102,400	-7.00%	$86,000
1993	$7,000	14.00%	$109,736	-4.00%	$75,560
1994	$7,000	13.00%	$117,002	21.00%	$84,427
1995	$7,000	23.00%	$136,912	-1.00%	$76,583
1996	$7,000	-4.00%	$124,435	10.00%	$77,241
1997	$7,000	10.00%	$129,879	-4.00%	$67,151
1998	$7,000	-1.00%	$121,581	23.00%	$75,596
1999	$7,000	21.00%	$140,113	13.00%	$78,423
2000	$7,000	-4.00%	$127,508	14.00%	$82,402
2001	$7,000	-7.00%	$112,528	9.90%	$83,586
2002	$7,000	0.05%	$105,411	0.05%	$76,565
2003	$7,000	7.20%	$106,000	7.20%	$75,077
2004	$7,000	11.50%	$111,190	11.50%	$76,711
2005	$7,000	16.30%	$122,314	16.30%	$82,215
2006	$7,000	10.30%	$127,913	10.30%	$83,683
2007	$7,000	3.00%	$124,750	3.00%	$79,194
2008	$7,000	-20.20%	$92,550	-20.20%	$56,197
2009	$7,000	20.20%	$104,246	20.20%	$60,548
2010	$7,000	6.40%	$103,917	6.40%	$57,423

At the end of 2010 there is a marked difference in the account values. In (C) Returns, where we had some negative results in the early years, the account value has been hampered all the way through to the end of 2010. The (B) Returns experience shows a comparative account value of $103,917. That is almost 81 per cent greater than the $57,423 account balance from the (C) Returns.

TABLE 4.9: 7% Withdrawal (Indexed @ 2.5%)

Year	Income	(B) Returns	(B) Account Value	(C) Returns	(C) Account Value
1992	$7,000	9.90%	$102,400	-7.00%	$86,000
1993	$7,175	14.00%	$109,561	-4.00%	$75,385
1994	$7,354	13.00%	$116,450	21.00%	$83,861
1995	$7,538	23.00%	$135,695	-1.00%	$75,485
1996	$7,726	-4.00%	$122,541	10.00%	$75,307
1997	$7,920	10.00%	$126,875	-4.00%	$64,375
1998	$8,118	-1.00%	$117,487	23.00%	$71,036
1999	$8,321	21.00%	$133,841	13.00%	$71,980
2000	$8,529	-4.00%	$119,958	14.00%	$73,529
2001	$8,742	-7.00%	$111,582	9.90%	$71,698
2002	$8,960	0.05%	$102,819	0.05%	$63,096
2003	$9,184	7.20%	$94,373	7.20%	$58,456
2004	$9,414	11.50%	$91,983	11.50%	$55,754
2005	$9,649	16.30%	$98,682	16.30%	$52,360
2006	$9,890	10.30%	$98,957	10.30%	$47,705
2007	$10,138	3.00%	$91,787	3.00%	$38,999
2008	$10,391	-20.20%	$72,033	-20.20%	$20,730
2009	$10,651	20.20%	$75,933	20.20%	$14,266
2010	$10,917	6.40%	$69,875	6.40%	$4,262

The same extended results we saw in Table 4.8 hold true when the 7 per cent withdrawal is indexed at 2.5 per cent per year. But in this scenario, where the negative returns occurred early ((C) Returns), we have basically exhausted the account.

TABLE 4.10: 5% Withdrawal

Year	Income	(B) Returns	(B) Account Value	(C) Returns	(C) Account Value
1992	$5,000	9.90%	$104,900	-7.00%	$88,000
1993	$5,000	14.00%	$114,586	-4.00%	$79,400
1994	$5,000	13.00%	$124,482	21.00%	$91,170
1995	$5,000	23.00%	$148,113	-1.00%	$85,259
1996	$5,000	-4.00%	$137,188	10.00%	$88,785
1997	$5,000	10.00%	$145,907	-4.00%	$80,233
1998	$5,000	-1.00%	$139,448	23.00%	$93,687
1999	$5,000	21.00%	$163,732	13.00%	$100,866
2000	$5,000	-4.00%	$152,183	14.00%	$109,988
2001	$5,000	-7.00%	$136,530	9.90%	$115,326
2002	$5,000	0.05%	$130,847	0.05%	$110,902
2003	$5,000	7.20%	$135,268	7.20%	$113,887
2004	$5,000	11.50%	$145,823	11.50%	$121,985
2005	$5,000	16.30%	$164,593	16.30%	$136,868
2006	$5,000	10.30%	$176,546	10.30%	$145,965
2007	$5,000	3.00%	$176,842	3.00%	$145,344
2008	$5,000	-20.20%	$136,120	-20.20%	$110,984
2009	$5,000	20.20%	$158,616	20.20%	$128,403
2010	$5,000	6.40%	$163,786	6.40%	$131,620

Here we have selected a 5 per cent instead of a 7 per cent withdrawal rate. On the surface, the respective high account balances may suggest that we are withdrawing too little. But the next Table 4.11 shows the impact of indexing this level of withdrawal at 2.5 per cent per year.

TABLE 4.11: 5% Withdrawal (Indexed @ 2.5%)

Year	Income	(B) Returns	(B) Account Value	(C) Returns	(C) Account Value
1992	$5,000	9.90%	$104,900	-7.00%	$88,000
1993	$5,125	14.00%	$114,161	-4.00%	$79,355
1994	$5,253	13.00%	$124,087	21.00%	$90,766
1995	$5,384	23.00%	$147,244	-1.00%	$84,474
1996	$5,519	-4.00%	$135,835	10.00%	$87,403
1997	$5,657	10.00%	$143,761	-4.00%	$78,250
1998	$5,798	-1.00%	$136,526	23.00%	$90,449
1999	$5,943	21.00%	$159,254	13.00%	$96,264
2000	$6,092	-4.00%	$146,791	14.00%	$103,650
2001	$6,244	-7.00%	$130,272	9.90%	$107,149
2002	$6,400	0.05%	$123,220	0.05%	$101,284
2003	$6,560	7.20%	$125,532	7.20%	$108,577
2004	$6,724	11.50%	$137,638	11.50%	$114,339
2005	$6,892	16.30%	$153,181	16.30%	$126,085
2006	$7,064	10.30%	$150,535	10.30%	$132,007
2007	$7,241	3.00%	$147,810	3.00%	$128,727
2008	$7,422	-20.20%	$110,530	-20.20%	$95,303
2009	$7,608	20.20%	$125,249	20.20%	$106,947
2010	$7,798	6.40%	$125,467	6.40%	$105,514

This example illustrates why carefully selecting your rate of withdrawal is so important. It also shows why I really prefer to keep withdrawals around a 5 per cent rate, which we can comfortably index. Even the negative scenario of the (C) Returns has not exhausted the account. At the same time, the lower withdrawal rate of 5 per cent, even when indexed, allows us to more readily cope with substantial market downturns such as those we saw in 2000, 2001 and 2008–2009. I know this example does not go back and review a hundred years of data, but it does use actual investment results and covers off a period of time when we have gone through two pretty sharp market downturns. Yes, negative returns at the outset of your withdrawal years can have a negative impact on your income-producing assets. But your ability to select a withdrawal rate in the 5 per cent range appears to moderate this potential problem.

Step 6. Assessing the Impact on Net Worth

The last of the six steps in the plan is to assess how the courses of action proposed in the blueprint will impact your income-producing assets. When I address this step in the planning work I do, I do not include other personal assets, such as home, cars, cottage et cetera. Other advisors might include these if they are trying to track total net worth, and that is fine. But within the sixth step, I want to keep this assessment strictly to those assets that are creating cash flow. By doing this, there are three key questions relating to the income-producing assets that you can examine.

First, given the assets you have and the withdrawals planned, are you maintaining, increasing or decreasing the value of these assets over time? Remember that overall projected rates of return for the portfolio are also going to enter into these projections. Different asset mixes will create different rates of return in illustrations. This is going to have a direct impact on the value of your investments.

Second, can you see a trend, over time, where the overall direction of the blueprint is allowing you to systematically convert fully-taxable assets into those that are more tax-efficient and/or non-taxable? If you look at the chart on the next page (Figure 4.12), you will see an example of where this has been the trend.

In this projection over a 30-year period, the income-producing assets show a definite shift in their value from very few non-registered assets at the outset to predominantly after-tax assets as we move out to age 90. Plus, in this particular example, the nominal value of the original assets has been maintained. That, in my opinion, is a very good direction to head.

The third question ties directly into the second one. Are you also reducing the overall tax liability to the estate through what has been proposed? As you can see from the line representing "net worth" in the chart below, this is clearly happening.

This is all part of capital preservation and wealth management.

FIGURE 4.12: Net Worth Projection

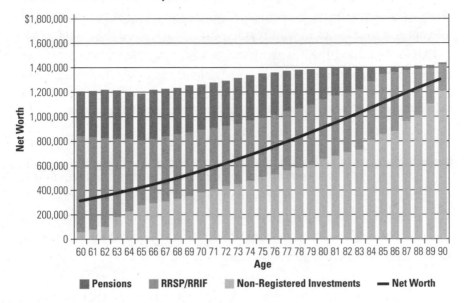

Annual Review Items

I want to wind up this section by talking about reviews of your blueprint. Hopefully I have been able to make the case that retirement income planning is a process and not a one-time event. Your blueprint is not a static document but rather one that is dynamic and changing. As such, at a review with your advisor, you need to address a number of items in addition to the investment statements. Those include the following:

- note changes in circumstances and changes in health
- define priorities/objectives for the next 12 months
- identify any "unique expenses" anticipated
- review any changes to income sources
- quantify existing payment amounts
- reaffirm cash flow needs
- revisit layering of income sources
- determine investments within the assets that are to be used to create income
- rebalance portfolio(s) if necessary

Review and communication are essential to make this process work efficiently. But please remember that this is a two-way responsibility. One of your responsibilities in your relationship with your advisor is to be proactive in contacting them when changes occur or when you simply have things that you wish to discuss.

MAKING YOUR BLUEPRINT WORK FOR YOU

1. Recognize that some of the objectives you have for your investments during your retirement are going to be conflicting. For example, you don't want to reduce the value of your income-producing assets, but you need to draw income out of them. Once again, in the withdrawal years, things are different.

2. Review the different models available, and try to get a sense for which planning model has greater appeal to you. This is a worthwhile assessment whether you are just about to start withdrawing your retirement income or if you have been withdrawing it for several years.

3. You have to pay attention to the withdrawal rate you are employing so that you can protect your income-producing assets. I have suggested that 5 per cent or slightly higher than that is comfortable. If you need to draw 7 per cent or more from your personal assets, you likely do not have a sufficient amount of capital to sustain that level of income over an extended period of time.

4. Be specific in designating the assets to be used to create payments through a process like the Cash Wedge. This can prevent the mistake of selling investments when they are down in value.

5. There are a large number of investment tools as your disposal. Sometimes by combining tools from the investment industry with those available in the insurance industry, the end result is more attractive and efficient than what could be obtained from the offerings of one industry alone.

6. Investment risk with the stock market is not the only risk-management issue. There are many others that can impact assets and income, including being too conservative with your investments.

7. Be sure to review your blueprint annually, so that any changes in circumstances can be addressed and incorporated into your blueprint.

PART
THREE

THE BUILDING MATERIALS

5

GOVERNMENT SOURCES OF INCOME

When you are going through your working years, your employment income is really your one source of cash flow. When you are retired, you may have six to eight different income streams. So which ones should you use first? How do you combine them to get the most effective results over time? There is an order in which income is most efficiently drawn. In this part of the book, I am going to take a closer look at the various sources of retirement income. They appear in the order in which I have found they are best engaged. Depending on your age when you retire, you initially may not have access to all sources of income, such as Old Age Security (OAS) and Canada Pension Plan (CPP). However, the objective is to use the least tax-efficient and least flexible sources of income first, as they become available.

Old Age Security (OAS)

I have always been (and still am) a strong believer that people should commence income from their government benefits as soon as they can. There are a number of reasons for this as I will discuss in this chapter. With OAS, there are no survivor benefits, no income-splitting opportunities, no flexibility, no option to commence this income prior to age 65 and it is fully taxable. For those reasons, I am listing it as the first layer of income.

OAS is a universal benefit for all Canadians (unless you are in prison). You don't make contributions to the OAS program as you do with the CPP. OAS is funded out of the general revenues of the federal government (otherwise known as tax revenue). The income is fully indexed to increases in the consumer price index (CPI), and adjustments are made on a quarterly basis. There are no reductions if the CPI declines. Monthly payments for the first quarter of 2011 are set at $524.23 for those entitled to the full pension.

What is meant by the "full pension"? Technically, there are 40 equal portions in the OAS "pie." Qualifying for the full pension allows you to receive all 40 portions each month. This amount is payable if you have lived in Canada for at least 40 years after turning 18, or if you meet all three of the following conditions:

1. You were born on or before July 1, 1952.
2. Between the time you turned 18 and July 1, 1977, you lived in Canada for some period of time.
3. You lived in Canada for the 10 years immediately before your application for OAS was approved.

If you do not meet the criteria in either of the full benefit categories, you may still be eligible for a partial pension. For example, someone who lived in Canada for 10 years would qualify for 10 of the 40 portions of the pie. In other words, he or she would have an entitlement to 25 per cent of the full pension.

It's Not a Clawback, It's a Social Benefit Repayment

The federal government determined that after reaching a certain level of net income ($67,668, including OAS payments from the previous year, in 2011) you did not "need" the full OAS pension. Every dollar of net income over $67,668 reduces the OAS amount by 15 per cent. Past a certain, higher net income level, it was determined that you did not need any OAS pension at all. As such, in 2011, when net income is $109,607 or above you will be ineligible for any OAS pension. This "means test" calculation is assessed on an individual income basis, not on household income. Since July 1996, OAS payments are adjusted based on the prior year's net income. There is no repayment of the benefit per se. It is simply adjusted or eliminated for the following year.

So that's fair and acceptable, right? After all, if you already have what is deemed to be more-than-sufficient means to retire comfortably, you shouldn't be too upset about having your OAS payments reduced or eliminated, should you? Well, if this is not happening to you, you might think it is no big deal. But let me share with you what is shared with me by retirees who are seeing a reduction or elimination of their OAS benefit: In almost all cases, it drives them crazy. After all, it is frustrating for them, after years of paying taxes, to forgo any of this payment.

So your net income comes into play and determines your level of entitlement to a government benefit. (More on net income in Part Four.) That is why you want to structure income in such a way as to keep the level of net income relatively low throughout retirement. In this way you will minimize the needless loss of government benefits and entitlements.

Payments to Canadian Non-Residents

If you no longer live in Canada, but lived here for at least 20 years after the age of 18, OAS payments will continue until your death, based on the same income conditions listed earlier. This also applies if you lived or worked in a country that has a social security agreement with Canada—because of that, you are considered to meet the 20-year residency requirement. If your residency in Canada was less than 20 years, payments are made to you for the month of departure and six months thereafter. Then they cease.

Annual updates for Old Age Security income payments and adjustments to the income levels used for calculating the social benefit repayment can be found at www.boomersblueprint.com.

Information on OAS supplemental programs, including the Guaranteed Income Supplement and the Spouse's Allowance, can be obtained at www.servicecanada.gc.ca.

The Canada Pension Plan (CPP/QPP)

The CPP retirement pension serves as the next layer of income that should be triggered. In this section, I will cover off some mechanics of the benefit and address the most common question people ask about their CPP pension, which is: Start now or start later? I also will describe the significant changes coming to CPP pension in 2012 and how this could possibly affect you going forward.

First, let's talk about how things will work up to the end of 2011, starting with how your CPP pension is calculated. The benefits payable are dependent upon the level of contributions made (by you and your employer) and the number of years during which they were made. This differs from OAS, which is a uniform amount with universal entitlement. The CPP is designed to replace about 25 per cent of the earnings from employment up to a maximum amount known as the yearly maximum pensionable earnings (YMPE).

In calculating your retirement benefit, 15 per cent of your lowest-earning years are removed from the calculation. This can provide a higher income if you have had lower or no earnings in certain years or if you were late in entering the workforce. There is also an adjustment for years when a parent was at home with children under the age of seven. In 2011, an individual aged 65 with entitlement to the maximum retirement benefit will receive a monthly CPP pension of $960.00.

Sharing Your CPP with Your Spouse

Sharing or assigning pensions allows spouses who are together (not separated or divorced) and who are both eligible, to combine their CPP pension incomes and split the total evenly between them. It is a form of income splitting and may offer you some tax savings, especially if there is a disparity in the amounts of CPP pension to which you and your spouse are entitled. The total pension entitlements for you and your spouse are added together and each of you receives payments for half of that amount. Each of you is responsible for paying tax on the portion you receive. Sharing CPP pensions results in an actual split of the payment when it is made. This is different from the pension splitting that is discussed in the section on taxation, where that split is accomplished at the time taxes are jointly filed.

In order to qualify to split CPP:

- both spouses must be at least age 60
- both must have applied for CPP retirement benefits if they were contributors (the splitting of income is allowed even if only one spouse has contributed—in those cases, the contributing spouse can apply)

The assignment of the pension income ceases:

- when one of the spouses dies
- upon divorce or after a separation of one year

Note: In the case of divorce or separation, benefits will revert to the original person who was entitled to them, but when the assignment ceases as a result of death, a survivor's income may be payable.

To split your CPP, you and your spouse need to apply together at a Service Canada office. You will be required to complete the request form, have the usual personal identification documents with you and present a marriage license or proof of cohabitation.

And When I Die . . .

A lump-sum benefit is payable to the estate or a representative of the estate on the death of a contributor. Currently this amount is a flat payment of $2,500. The Quebec Pension Plan (QPP) pays six times the monthly receipt of the pension, to a maximum of $2,500. Oh yes, before I forget to mention it, this is a taxable benefit.

Surviving spouse's pension

For your survivor to be eligible for CPP survivor benefits, you must have contributed in:

- one-third of the calendar years in your contributory period, or
- 10 calendar years, whichever is less, but
- not less than three years

In determining the survivor's benefit, the following factors are considered:

- the spouse's age at the time the contributor died
- how long and how much the contributor paid into the plan
- whether the spouse is already receiving a CPP disability or retirement benefit
- whether he or she has dependent children
- whether he or she has a disability

CPP calculates what the pension entitlement of the deceased contributor would have been if they were 65 at the time of their death. This factor is combined with the age of the surviving spouse at the time of the contributor's death.

Additional Survivor Benefit Points

- There is an additional benefit to the survivor calculated for children who are under the age of 18 and for those between ages 18 and 25 if they are attending a recognized educational institution.
- If more than one survivor benefit is payable, only the greater benefit will be paid.
- Survivor benefits do not end on remarriage.
- A spouse already in receipt of a CPP retirement income can collect the survivor benefit as well. The sum of the two receipts cannot exceed the maximum income payable to a pensioner aged 65.

Pay particular attention to the last point above. It is going to have meaningful and direct bearing on recommendations that are going to be made regarding your CPP benefits.

Full details on survivors' and children's benefits can be found at http://www.servicecanada.gc.ca/eng/isp/pub/cpp/survivor/survivor.pdf.

Sooner or Later? Early Receipt of CPP

Of all the retirement income planning issues, I don't think that there is a question I am more commonly asked than: Should I take my Canada Pension benefit early or wait until I am 65? So, let's start by looking at what has to happen under 2011 rules in order for you to commence your benefit. You must be at least age 60 and:

- have stopped working, or
- continue working but meet the "work cessation test," which means:
  - no employment income for one month, or
  - having employment income that is less than the maximum monthly CPP retirement benefit ($960.00 in 2011) for two consecutive months

These rules apply until the start of 2012, at which time they will change. See "The New CPP Rules for 2012" later in this chapter.

Remember the first rule in layering your income—use the least tax-efficient and least-flexible sources of income first. The CPP follows right behind OAS in that regard. Since CPP is available prior to age 65, my recommendation is to start it as soon as you can. If you are retired, take the CPP payment rather than use your own personal assets to generate that income.

The rules in effect to the end of 2011 reduce your CPP retirement income by 0.5 per cent for every month that you commence it prior to age 65. In other words, someone starting at age 60 would be in receipt of payment 60 months before their 65th birthday. So their payment would be 30 per cent less (60 x 0.5 per cent) than if they waited until age 65. The effect of this is shown in Figure 5.1 below. At first glance, the lower initial income may make you feel like you are being penalized for starting before age 65. After all, the table shows a payment of $672 at age 60 compared to $960 at age 65.

But here are the other considerations. First, by Service Canada calculations, the crossover age wherein the total receipts are "even" for someone taking reduced income at age 60 and someone starting their full entitlement at age 65 is at age 76.7. While I hope that all of my clients live well past that age, the fact is that some will and some won't. Also, this is a simple calculation and does not factor in the time value of money, which simply means that a dollar today has more value than a dollar paid to you five years from now. If you want to test this out, borrow some money from a friend and tell them that you will pay them back the same amount five years from now. See how happy they are with that suggestion. It works the same way here with earlier versus deferred pension payments. Including the time value adjustment of those earlier payments would move the crossover closer to age 80.

Second, in our example, the retiree would have had 60 months' worth of payments of $672 between age 60 and 65. That is a total of $40,320 over those five years. On the surface, starting early may look like a penalty, but don't view it that way. Look at it as an early enhancement to your cash flow, as shown in Table 5.1, assuming entitlement to the maximum benefit at 65.

TABLE 5.1: CCP Payment and Crossover Changes

Age	2011 Adjustment	2011 Income	Crossover Age 2011	2016 Income*	Crossover Age 2016
60	-30%	$672	76.7	$614	73.9
61	-24%	$730	77.7	$683	74.9
62	-18%	$787	78.7	$753	75.9
63	-12%	$845	79.7	$822	76.9
64	-6%	$902	80.7	$893	77.9
65	0%	$960		$960	
66	6.84%	$1,026	81.7	$1,040	76.9
67	13.68%	$1,091	81.7	$1,121	76.9
68	20.52%	$1,157	81.7	$1,202	76.9
69	27.36%	$1,223	81.7	$1,283	76.9
70	34.20%	$1,288	81.7	$1,363	76.9

* Projected for comparative purposes using 2011 payment rates

Other Reasons Why I Have Promoted Early Receipt of Pension

Planning recommendations can only appropriately be made after assessing all of the details in any particular situation. However, I have found that generally it has been beneficial to start CPP retirement benefits early, especially in the context of a couple in a two-income household. The reasons for this are as follows:

1. There is no capital value of government benefits to the estate other than a $2,500 taxable death benefit. In other words, there is no future estate benefit that you preserve by starting later.

2. If the CPP income is taken and not required for cash flow purposes, it could be directed into an RRSP if there was contribution room. If there was no RRSP contribution room available, the after-tax amount of the payment could be placed into a Tax-Free Savings Account (TFSA). However, if there was no RRSP contribution room available, I would seldom advise triggering the benefit if the additional income from CPP would put you into a higher tax bracket. These actions allow the annuitant to create a more flexible asset from the CPP cash flow, which can be used when they actually retire. In addition, since the recipient is no longer able to contribute to CPP, they could now direct what would have been their CPP contributions to an RRSP or other savings vehicle. These contribution rules will be changing in 2012.

3. By starting early, there is a very strong likelihood that, in the case of a married couple, there will be a "topping up" of the reduced retirement benefit through the addition of a survivor's benefit. The formula allows for a plan member to receive both a retirement and survivor's benefit, but the sum of those two payments cannot exceed the maximum retirement benefit for a pensioner aged 65 ($960 in 2011). But let's consider a couple, both of whom are entitled to the maximum retirement pension and both of whom wait until age 65 to commence the CPP benefit. Basically, the survivor will never receive a survivor's benefit because each of them are already at the maximum retirement entitlement.

4. You may already be entitled to the maximum benefit you can receive at age 65, but are still making contributions. It works that way with any type of defined benefit pension plan where you have participated for an extended period.

About the only potential downside I can see to commencing the retirement benefit early is if the pensioner becomes disabled between age 60 and 65 (because the disability benefit would be higher). You are not permitted to switch to a disability benefit after the retirement benefit has commenced. As is the case with so many considerations in retirement, your state of health at the time is a definite factor.

The New CPP Rules for 2012

Starting in 2012, there will be four key changes to the Canada Pension Plan. The changes will be phased in starting in 2012 and will be fully implemented by 2016.

First, there is a positive change in the calculation of career earnings. Simply stated, by increasing the dropout percentage for years of low or no earnings from the current 15 per cent of average career earnings to 16 per cent in 2012 and 17 per cent in 2014, you should have a higher retirement benefit when you elect to receive it.

Second, the removal of the work cessation test is a welcome end to this unnecessary annoyance. You will no longer be required to cease employment or have a reduced income for a two-month period in order to be eligible to apply for your benefit.

The above two amendments are constructive, but the following two amendments create very significant changes for those who wish to take their retirement benefits prior to age 65 and particularly for those who are earning employment income during this period.

The third proposed change will further reduce the payments for those who start before 65 and further enhance them for those who start after 65. From a practical and actuarial perspective, these adjustments are appropriate given the longer life expectancy of today's retirees compared to those who retired 20 years ago.

When fully implemented, the early receipt reduction per month will be 0.6 per cent compared to the 0.5 per cent that it is in 2011. The changes for delaying receipt will start in 2011 and be fully in place by 2013. Table 5.2 on the next page illustrates how these changes will be phased in over the next three and five years respectively. I have shown the reductions and increases by percentages. If you refer back to Table 5.1, you will see how this would look in terms of dollars, using 2011 payment rates.

I want to use an example just to avoid confusion with these numbers. Assume that you are entitled to the maximum pension at 65 and that you commence the benefit early at age 60, in 2013. Your maximum payment would be reduced by 32.40 per cent. After you start, you are not affected by any other changes that you see in this table.

TABLE 5.2: How the CPP Changes Will Be Phased In

Age at Start	2011	2012	2013	2014	2015	2016 Onward
60	-30%	-31.20%	-32.40%	-33.60%	-34.80%	-36.00%
61	-24%	-24.96%	-25.92%	-26.88%	-27.84%	-28.80%
62	-18%	-18.72%	-19.44%	-20.16%	-20.88%	-21.60%
63	-12%	-12.48%	-12.96%	-13.44%	-13.92%	-14.40%
64	-6%	-6.24%	-6.48%	-7.28%	-6.96%	-7.20%
65	0%	0%	0%	0%	0%	0%
66	6.84%	7.68%	8.40%	8.40%	8.40%	8.40%
67	13.68%	15.36%	16.80%	16.80%	16.80%	16.80%
68	20.52%	23.04%	25.20%	25.20%	25.20%	25.20%
69	27.36%	30.72%	33.60%	33.60%	33.60%	33.60%
70	34.20%	38.40%	42.00%	42.00%	42.00%	42.00%

The fourth and most problematic (in my opinion) amendment is that those under the age of 65 who have earned (employment) income while in receipt of the CPP retirement benefit will now be required to make contributions to the plan. CPP contends that they are implementing these changes to help retirees in many different scenarios more effectively transition into retirement while they are still working. They are also promoting this as a way for pensioners to increase their CPP benefit through additional contributions to the plan while they are in receipt of the retirement benefit.

This is being called the Post Retirement Benefit (PRB). It will be an option if you are working beyond age 65 but a requirement before that age. Contribution rates will remain the same and the increase to pension income will be applied the following year. The amount of increased benefit is equal to 1/40th of the maximum payment for a retiree aged 65. This does not come into effect until 2012, but here is an estimate of how the numbers will look if we use 2011 figures and assume employment income at or over the YMPE.

Yearly Maximum Pensionable Earnings (YMPE) $48,300.00
Total CPP contributions, employee and employer $ 4,435.20
Maximum monthly benefit for pensioner age 65 $ 960.00
Increase in pension for the following year $ 288.00 ($24.00/month)

Contributions and the resulting PRB benefits for employment incomes that are less than the YMPE will be on a proportionate basis.

It is this feature that has me distressed about the changes. Many retirees are using early CPP to transition into retirement while they continue to work. The new rules would require continued contributions to the plan. Not only does this encroach upon the cash flow of the pensioner, but it also means that now employers have to contribute for this individual. That was an advantage that current pensioners had. They could be employed and neither they nor the employer were required to make CPP contributions (in fact they are not permitted to do so).

Further to this, many retirees leave their formal career and choose to work on their own through contract or consulting work. This change now means that if they are taking CPP and are under the age of 65, they will end up paying both the employee and employer portions of the contribution ($4,435.2 using 2011 figures). The biggest concern out of all of this is that it will apply to all pensioners under the age of 65, regardless of when they commenced their retirement benefit. So if you started CPP in 2009 while still working, are under the age of 65 in 2012 and have employment income, you will be required to start making contributions to the plan. This will be the case even if you had not been making contributions for the last two or three years. This marks the first time that I have ever seen a change in a government program where those who were already participating in the benefit were not "grandfathered" under what were the existing rules.

So, Should You Still Consider Taking Your Benefit Early?

The reasons why I promote taking this benefit early were listed previously. What will be different under the new rules? The reduction for early receipt will be higher, which means the crossover will occur sooner. If you are receiving CPP pension, have employment income and are under the age of 65, you will now have to contribute to the plan. But that would be true if you were working, whether or not you were in receipt of the pension. So if you are already at the maximum entitlement, you may as well take the pension, so that any new contributions are creating the PRB you would otherwise not get.

I have read some other thoughts on this topic, some of which suggest deferring your CPP pension all the way to age 70. This would increase your pension to 142 per cent of what would be paid to a pensioner at age 65. The reasoning behind this suggestion was that once you pass the crossover age in your mid to late seventies, there is a large difference in the sum of payments to age 90 and beyond for those who delay commencement. For that argument to have merit, you have to assume that you are going to live well beyond the average life expectancy. It also means using your survivor-friendly and estate-creating assets first and depleting them until you can start your higher CPP income at age 70. And remember that your CPP basically ends when you do and has no estate value. By deferring your CPP pension you would be creating an inflexible, higher and fully-taxable income stream at age 70. If you have also deferred using your RRSP accounts, you may find that you have a very high level of taxable income at age 71, with no ability to control it. Neither of these points makes any sense at all and they are in complete conflict with the objectives of the Income Continuum.

Again, every situation needs to be evaluated on its own merits. But after very careful assessment, even if all of the changes were in place, I still feel that the reasons why you should start this benefit earlier outweigh the potential for higher income later. Search for reasons to convince yourself not to take your benefit early and see if you can find any that are that compelling. I will be taking mine as soon as it is available.

Annual updates for CPP benefits are available at www.boomersblue print.com.

MAKING YOUR BLUEPRINT WORK FOR YOU

1. The Old Age Security (OAS) benefit is "means tested." This means that once your net income exceeds a certain level, your benefits are reduced and ultimately eliminated. That is one of the reasons why you need to have an awareness of what your levels of net income will be today and in the future.

2. While every situation needs to be evaluated on its own merits, there are quite a number of reasons why it makes sense to start your CPP retirement benefit early. But you need to assess whether or not there is merit to do so in your own situation. With both OAS and CPP it makes far more sense to use those sources of income before tapping into your own personal assets.

3. The new CPP rules that start in 2012 provide greater reductions in monthly income for starting early and larger payments should you defer commencement. Don't be fooled by what you see on the surface. Look closely at how this impacts you and, if applicable, your spouse or partner.

6

CORPORATE SOURCES OF INCOME

Employment Income

I know what some of you are thinking, "Employment income? I thought I was retiring!" But often people like to be involved in some kind of employment after they retire. There are a number of reasons that drive this decision. The obvious one is the financial rewards. Less income needs to be drawn from assets if you are receiving a paycheque. This has the added benefit of allowing assets to grow or to at least be drawn upon in a lesser amount. Income earned from employment may go toward a special purchase, such as a vacation. Post-retirement work can be a form of social activity or recreation. It may also be an opportunity to be involved in an area of personal interest.

Work after retirement does not necessarily mean full-time employment. There are many part-time, contract, casual and consulting opportunities available. Most retirees, if they decide to work, will do so on a schedule and a basis that is convenient for them.

The 8th annual Rethink Retirement™ survey conducted by Desjardins Financial Security re-affirmed the notion that "retirement ain't what it used to be." The old paradigm of retirement saw people go from full-time work to complete retirement. Today, more and more are taking a different approach and transitioning from their work life into retirement.

According to the survey:

- 16 per cent of retirees continue gainful employment.
- 8 per cent of today's workers (including partial retirees) were once fully retired before returning to work. This proportion rises to 42 per cent among partial retirees.
- The main reasons for going back to work: needing more money for personal projects (46 per cent) and wanting to counter the negative effects of an economic situation on retirement income (29 per cent).

Findings reprinted with Desjardins' permission

Some people may simply have a desire to make a more gradual transition into a full state of non-employment as discussed in Part One of this book. Some find the adjustment to full retirement too abrupt and go back to some form of work. And yes, there are some people who don't wish to retire at any point in time. The entertainment and business world are rife with such examples. On this point, the legendary George Burns said, "Retirement at sixty-five is ridiculous. When I was sixty-five I still had pimples."

I said that I was going to examine these various sources of income in the order that they should be used to create the cash flow needed in retirement. So why would employment income not be the first layer? It may very well be if the retiree is not at the age to trigger income from government benefits. But as discussed, if they are entitled to CPP and/or OAS, those would almost always be the first layers of income.

Pensions

So far I have suggested that government benefits should be your first layers of cash flow as soon as they are available. The next source is employment income and now we arrive at pensions. If you or your spouse do not have a pension benefit, you may wish to skip this section.

A pension plan can be an effective accumulation vehicle since it involves matching employer contributions, but contribution formulas and types of pension plans vary substantially. It is very important for you to be aware of the amount of income that you can realistically expect from this source. In addition, we are living and working in a time where it is common for people to move from one job or career to another. This obviously has an impact on the ability to build long-term values and income in a pension plan.

Types of Pensions

I would like to use this book to talk about the use of your pension plan in terms of income or using the value of your plan rather than the mechanics of the accumulation vehicle itself. That said, I do feel it necessary to include a very cursory overview of the two types of pension plans that are out there and some of their distinguishing features.

When all is said and done, there are just two types of pension plans, defined benefit and defined contribution. Here is the best way to explain the differences between the two, and it involves Sam and Dave, who are the best of friends. On a hot summer day, they step up to the windows at the local dairy bar to order an ice cream cone. Sam says, "I'll have a large cone, please." The server brings him what he requested, and as he hands it to Sam, he asks him for $2.75. Sam knew what he was going to receive when the cone came to the window. He was going to get a large cone, although he did not know how much it was going to cost him. That is like a defined benefit pension. Employees prefer these types of plans because the income that this type of plan will provide to them (benefit) is known (defined). But this type of pension is expensive for the employer to fund and the costs to the employer are undefined. This is why we see more and more private employers moving away from funding this type of plan.

Dave, at the other window, reaches into his pocket and finds that he has only $2.00 with him. He asks his server, "Can I have whatever size cone this $2.00 will buy for me?" And the server returns with what can be purchased for that amount of money. Dave's situation reflects the mechanics of a defined contribution pension. He knew exactly what the cost was going to be, but he was not sure what his benefit was going to look like until it arrived at the window. Participants in a defined contribution (also known as a "money purchase") pension have a similar experience.

This is a snapshot of the pension landscape in Canada, as reported by the *Globe and Mail* in October 2009:

- 84 per cent of public service workers have pension plans
- 78 per cent of these plans are indexed defined benefit plans
- 25 per cent of private sector workers have a pension plan
- 18 per cent of these plans are defined benefit plans
- 11 million workers (60 per cent of Canada's workers) have no pension plan at all
- 8 million (45 per cent of Canada's workers) have no pension plan or RRSPs

What this tells you is that if you are in a defined benefit pension, you are truly part of a minority in Canada. It also shows the disparity between the public and private sector in terms of pension benefits.

Defined Benefit Pension Plans

As the name of suggests, there is a specific formula that determines what the plan members' financial benefit will be at retirement. As such, the amount of income to be paid out by the plan is known in advance. A number of different formulas can be used to calculate the income payable, but regardless of the calculations used, there are three key factors that will determine the retirement income to be received:

1. years of pensionable service
2. the defined pension benefit factor, which is usually between 1 and 2 per cent per year of service
3. a formula to measure your income, such as career average earnings or final average earnings (e.g., the best five years of income in the last seven years of service)

Integrated benefits

This option allows the pensioner to take into account the amount of government payments they will ultimately receive and combine those with their pension in order to provide a higher income earlier. This has the effect of levelling the total pension income, except for any indexing provisions.

FIGURE 6.1: Integrated Benefits

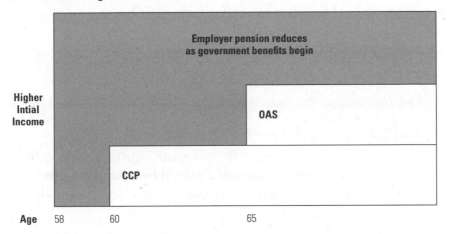

At the time the CPP/OAS benefits commence, the employment pension is reduced by roughly the same dollar amount. The trade-off for this higher initial income is that there is no increase to the overall retirement income at the time CPP and OAS commence. If this option is available, it will be included in your statement of pension options.

Bridging

Bridge benefits, unlike integrated benefits, are paid after early retirement commences until the plan member turns age 65 and can collect OAS and full CPP/QPP retirement benefits. The employer pension does not decline, and the full benefits of CPP/QPP and OAS are paid in addition to the pension income. The bridge is an additional payment, provided by the employer, that does not impact the future value of the pension income or government entitlements.

Indexation

These are adjustments made to the amount of pension income to allow it to keep pace with inflation. Indexing formulas vary. Normally they are stated as a goal rather than a commitment, and often the target amount of indexing will be a fraction or percentage of the actual inflation rate. Application of the indexing feature in whole or in part will be contingent on the overall health of the plan, including actuarial soundness, surpluses et cetera. This benefit is most common in public sector plans and is very seldom found in the private sector. Bridging and benefit integration are enhancements found only in defined benefit plans. And defined benefit plans are the only form of pension that may provide indexation of benefits.

Defined Contribution (Money Purchase) Plans

The other pension plan option is far less complicated than the defined benefit model. In a defined contribution plan, the employee, employer or both contribute a fixed percentage of income. Usually, but not always, the amount of contribution is the same from both parties.

The account value of these plans is the combination of employee and employer contributions plus investment growth (or loss). Assuming any vesting requirements have been satisfied, the employee is entitled to the account value to create his or her retirement income.

Employers are moving away from the defined benefit form of pension since their liabilities are undefined. With a defined contribution model, they know exactly what their costs will be. By moving to a defined contribution arrangement, the responsibility for retirement planning now shifts to the employee. The employee chooses how the pension money will be invested, and will need to do some planning around what may or may not be successfully provided by the pension plan. And therein is one of the big problems for the employee. Although the defined contribution plan provides more choices and more flexibility for the plan member, it may not be easy for them to know what kind of income is going to be delivered from this plan when they retire.

There are also employment situations today where both types of pension plan exist. Normally what has happened in these situations is that the employer has decided to "cap" and move away from the defined benefit plan and have all new contributions go into a defined contribution arrangement.

What Does Your Pension Statement Tell You?

As a member of a pension plan, you will receive an annual statement. In the case of a defined contribution plan, the account balance of the pension plan will be shown along with activity for the year, such as contributions and investment results. There may also be a commuted benefit value in the event of termination and an amount that would be payable in the event of the plan member's death. Since you are dealing with a value in an account, you should get some idea of what this is going to mean in terms of income. There may be tools on the plan provider's website to assist you with this. You may also find that it is beneficial to have an advisor help you with your projections and include all of the other potential sources of income you expect to have or to create.

Defined benefit plan statements often include the same information listed above and will show the pension earned to date that will apply at the normal retirement date, usually age 65. What you should know is that the future monthly income amount that is shown on your pension statement will quite likely not be the amount that you receive. Why is that? The annual statement of a defined benefit plan commonly projects the future income payable on the basis of a single life annuity with a five-year guarantee. What you need to be aware of is how this income is calculated. As you will see in the pages that follow, if you choose a joint life annuity, a longer guarantee period or both, your actual pension payable may be 15 to 25 per cent lower than the amount shown on your statement.

Since pension benefits can represent a large percentage of your retirement income, such a reduction could have a major impact on your plans. Discuss this with your advisor. Understand what it is that you can ultimately expect from your pension. Providing your advisor with both a recent statement and your benefits and pension booklet is helpful, but if you can obtain a projection of income options from your human resources department, that is even better.

Income from Your Pension

You contribute to your pension plan to accumulate funds for your retirement. When the time comes to create income from this asset, the role of the pension plan actually ceases. Regardless of whether you have a defined benefit or a defined contribution plan, there are basically two options to commence income from your pension plan:

- a life annuity, or
- a life income fund

Your income can be created directly through a life annuity that is purchased with your plan proceeds. This provides the monthly payment that most people simply refer to as "my pension." Or you can move your fund out of your pension plan (known as "commuting your pension accumulation") into a Life Income Fund (LIF) or a Restricted Life Income Fund (RLIF), which are based on provincial or federal legislation respectively. We will deal with each of these options separately.

Pension Income Option One: Life Annuities

Until the early 1990s, the life annuity was the most common, and to a large extent the only, option for commencing income from a pension plan or locked-in asset. A life annuity is a stream of future payments composed of a combination of principal and interest.

Think of an annuity as a loan in reverse. When you borrow money, you arrange a repayment schedule of so much per month until the principal and interest are completely paid off. With a life annuity, instead of borrowing capital, you are lending your pension plan value to the institution or plan trustees. They repay you on a monthly basis. That is your pension income. Instead of a set period of time for repayment, as you are used to when you borrow money, the income schedule for a life annuity is based upon average life expectancy. Some individuals pass away before average life expectancy and "subsidize" the payments for those people who live longer than the average.

When you leave your employment, your pension may commence immediately or you may elect to defer it to start at a later time. Why would someone choose to defer it? Not everyone leaves their formal employment and enters into full retirement. There may be a period of transition in another employment role where you don't want to have pension income in addition to employment income. There will also be an increase in the amount of income that the pension will provide if it does not start for several years.

Remember that you can never outlive the income to be paid to you from a life annuity. Regardless of how long you live, the income will be paid. In a very real sense, you are purchasing your income with the capital accumulating in the plan.

Life Annuity Options

There are different forms of life annuities and various features that apply to each of them. This recognizes that pension plan members have different financial circumstances and objectives. When the time comes for you to assess your pension options, there are a number of decisions that you must make in choosing your lifetime income. To give this section some real meaning for you, let's use a sample Pension Options quotation to connect descriptions and numbers as we discuss the various annuity features.

Here are the assumptions for the quotation. Employee Jack is a male age 62. His spouse, Diane, is 61. His pension account value is $500,000. Income is to commence one month from now. Here are the pension income (annuity) options from which Jack could make his choice. This quote was prepared using annuity rates in effect in December 2010.

TABLE 6.2: Pension Income Options

Option*	Annuitant Income	Survivor Income
Single Life G5	$2,710	n/a
Single Life G10	$2,643	n/a
Single Life G15	$2,557	n/a
Joint Life 66 2/3 G5	$2,391	$1,602
Joint Life 66 2/3 G10	$2,372	$1,589
Joint Life 66 2/3 G15	$2,344	$1,570
Joint Life 100 G5	$2,270	$2,270
Joint Life 100 G10	$2,268	$2,268
Joint Life 100 G15	$2,259	$2,259

*G refers to the guarantee period.

Single or joint life

Jack can choose a life annuity based on his life only (single life annuity) or one that would pay a benefit for as long as either he or Diane is alive (joint life annuity). Normally, if a single life annuity is chosen, a guarantee period is attached in order to provide both some form of income continuance to a survivor and some potential estate benefit. The highest income shown on the quotation page is for a single life annuity based on Jack's life only. If Diane had her own pension and there were other assets to create income, then perhaps a single life annuity would be worthy of consideration. I am going to assume that Jack wants to make sure there is some survivor income for Diane without any time limits, so that eliminates the first three options from their quote.

Level or reducing survivor income

Jack and Diane have decided that a joint life annuity is the appropriate choice for them. The income to Jack will stay level for his life. Income for a surviving annuitant can be level or it can reduce by 25 per cent, 33 per cent or 50 per cent. Options 4 through 6 show a survivor income to Diane based on 66 2/3 of what was being paid to Jack. The remaining quotes show a survivor income that is level, or 100 per cent of Jack's payment. In many, but not all, annuities, the reduction in the survivor's income does not occur until the end of what is called the "guarantee period," which will be discussed next.

   Is a reducing survivor benefit an appropriate choice or should it always be level? Just like the decision between single or joint life, the answer depends on a number of factors, many of which are financial. Consider the following. Are there other assets that can replace the income reduction should Jack pass away first? We know the age difference between Jack and Diane, but what is it in your situation? What is the state of health of each person? No decision about income and assets, especially involving your pension, should be made without full consideration of the big picture. This is yet another reason why you need to consolidate your holdings with one advisor at this time in your life in order to make most efficient use of all of your assets.

Guarantee period

Jack and Diane have decided on a joint life annuity with level income to the survivor. This means that they have narrowed their options to 7, 8 or 9. To finish making their choice, they simply have to conclude what they would like to choose as a guarantee period for this annuity. Think of the guarantee period like a warranty on a new toaster or car. Basically, it provides repair or reconciliation should something happen early in the life of your purchase. The same applies to an annuity. The guarantee assures that a certain value will be paid out either in the form of income, balance of payments to the estate or both.

Let's use the example of the joint life level income annuity with a 15-year guarantee in Option 9. Jack is the pension plan member and Diane is the joint annuitant. Exactly five years after the annuity starts, Jack passes away. Since they chose a level income option for the survivor, Diane now receives the same amount of income that Jack had been receiving. She passes away exactly five years from the date of Jack's passing. In total, 10 years' worth of payments have been made. The 15-year guarantee means that five years' worth of income payments would be paid to the estate since both annuitants passed away within 15 years of starting the annuity. If either of them had lived past 15 years and then passed away, there would be no residual payment to the estate. When you look at the difference in monthly incomes for options 7, 8 and 9, the addition of a guarantee period is really a very inexpensive form of insurance.

The guarantee period is a totally separate issue from the fact that the income is guaranteed for life. Whether a single or joint life annuity is elected, it is prudent to attach a guarantee period. The guarantee period can be 5 to 15 years for pension-source annuities and, when added to the age of the plan holder, cannot exceed the number 90. Alternatively, the calculation may use the age of the spouse. This issue does not have much application for someone age 65, but if the pensioner is converting any registered account to a life annuity at an older age, it may be a factor.

The guarantee period may serve to:

- provide a time period during which benefits could continue to a survivor

- ensure that a reduced benefit does not come into effect for a speci-
  fied time frame (check your annuity contract for this provision)
- ensure that a minimum number of payments will be paid either to
  the pensioner, their survivor(s) or the estate rather than left with
  the trustee or insurer
- provide a lump-sum payment of unused pension values to the
  estate in the event of the early passing of a pensioner and spouse

Your employer pension options may or may not have guarantees attached
to them. This is worth looking into and may have a significant impact on
your ultimate decision regarding what you do with your pension asset
at retirement. You may find that if none of the annuity choices offered
has all of the features you want, it may be better to purchase the annuity
outside of the plan in order to obtain the guarantees you feel are important. Normally, but not always, the income from the plan will be slightly
higher than the level of income that can be obtained in the marketplace.
It is also very important to be aware that only formal annuity payments
from the pension plan are considered eligible pension income for purposes of benefitting from the pension credit and for pension splitting
under the age of 65.

Choosing your life annuity option

For most people with long tenure in a pension plan, their entitlement is the
largest single asset they own. As such, what to do with that asset becomes
the biggest financial decision they will ever have to make. (Don't confuse
that with the decision to have children, which is also a huge financial
decision. Making the kids was far more fun than making pension contributions.) Once the form of pension income (annuity) is chosen, it cannot be
changed, so it is very important to ensure that care is taken when making
this decision. Some of the important considerations include:

- What is the state of health of you and your spouse?
- What are the survivor needs of your spouse?
- Is your spouse also in a pension plan?
- What other income-producing assets do you have?

- What is your timing like? Are you locking in long-term annuity rates at a time when interest rates are at historical lows?
- Is it your desire to generate some estate value from your pension?
- Do you have or could you acquire enough life insurance to replace all or part of your pension income?

As stated before, the more guarantees you attach to your income option, the lower the income amount. Like our loan-in-reverse analogy, if we ask to pay it back over a longer term, the payment goes down. The same thing happens to an annuity when more guarantees are put in place. You may recall the point I was making earlier on reading your pension statement. Jack may have been thinking all along, based on what his pension statement showed, that he was going to have a retirement income from his pension of $2,710 per month. The normal form of pension usually illustrated on a statement is a single life annuity guaranteed for five years. But after deciding on a joint life annuity with a 15-year guarantee period, that monthly income is actually going to be $2,259 per month. That is a difference of $451 per month or about 16.67 per cent less, for life.

Pension Income Option Two: Life Income Fund (LIF)

The second option for creating income from your pension plan is to "commute" its value. When the proceeds of your pension account are moved into a locked-in plan, it is referred to as "commuting your pension." Funds that are governed by provincial legislation can be moved into a locked-in retirement account (LIRA), which can be converted into a LIF or LRIF account (depending on the province) when income is required. Federally governed funds can be commuted into a locked-in RRSP, which is converted into an RLIF for income creation.

The features of these different plans are similar enough that I am taking the liberty of focusing on the LIRA/LIF just to save going back and forth among these income vehicles. This is intended to be a general description. In addition, legislation varies by province and federally. Make sure that you know what governing jurisdiction applies to your account. A summary table of provincial legislation can be found in the Appendix.

So how does the LIF work, how does it compare to a life annuity and why might you choose one over the other, or even a combination of the two? Let's revisit the pension options for Jack and Diane and see how these options compare.

When you elect an annuity with your pension accumulation, you are purchasing income with the value of your pension account. With a LIF, you are moving the value of your pension account (commuted value) to a personally owned vehicle from which you will draw an income. The commuted value of Jack's account is $500,000 and, for the purpose of making valid comparisons, we will assume that all of this account can be moved to a LIF on a tax-sheltered basis (more on this later).

Lump-sum withdrawals are not permitted from your LIF account (except in cases involving extreme financial hardship or terminal illness). But, the income from your LIF can be quite flexible. There is a minimum income that must be paid out from a LIF on an annual basis. LIFs follow the same minimum withdrawal formula that applies to RRIF accounts (detailed in Chapter 7). Income from a pension must, by law, provide payments for the lifetime of the pension plan member. As such, there is also a maximum income that is permitted to be paid. You may elect an income anywhere between the minimum and maximum. You also have the option to change the amount of income at any time. The maximum income that can be removed from a LIF is based upon several factors, including:

1. your age on January 1 and the maximum withdrawal percentage that applies to the jurisdictional legislation of your LIF (see Figure 6.3)
2. the value of your LIF account on January 1
3. the CANSIM rate (which is the rolling 10-year average on the Government of Canada 10-year bond or 6 per cent, whichever is greater)

The determination of which province's pension laws apply to locked-in pension money is based on which province the person was working in when his or her employment ended, rather than on the location of the institution holding the money, the person's subsequent place of residence or where the pension plan is registered (unless federally registered).

TABLE 6.3: LIF Maximum Withdrawal Percentages (Example)

Age on Jan. 1	Max %	Age on Jan. 1	Max %	Age on Jan. 1	Max %	Age on Jan. 1	Max %
50	6.27	60	6.85	70	8.22	80	12.82
51	6.31	61	6.94	71	8.45	81	13.87
52	6.35	62	7.04	72	8.71	82	15.19
53	6.40	63	7.14	73	9.00	83	16.90
54	6.45	64	7.26	74	9.34	84	19.18
55	6.51	65	7.38	75	9.71	85	20.00
56	6.57	66	7.52	76	10.15		
57	6.63	67	7.67	77	10.66		
58	6.70	68	7.83	78	11.25		
59	6.77	69	8.02	79	11.96		

(Earliest purchase age and withdrawal rates vary by province)

To determine Jack's potential income from a LIF, I will use a LIF calculator. You can find a link to calculate your potential LIF income at www.boomersblueprint.com.

The monthly income for Jack's first year is calculated to be $2,460. But remember that the maximum withdrawal amount is recalculated every year. So before we compare the LIF option to his life annuity quotes, let's take an extended look at Jack's LIF, in different investment scenarios at selected ages.

Several things are revealed in Table 6.4. First, the obvious point—the better your rate of investment return, the better your income and the higher the account value. Conversely, a lower return on your account can decrease your income over time. One of the issues then for choosing investments within your LIF portfolio is to be careful in terms of how conservative you wish to be. Being overly conservative may result in a continually declining portfolio. A second observation is that in every scenario the incomes and the account values eventually decline. More than anything else, this shows the impact of the minimum withdrawal formula, which eventually requires that larger and larger percentages of the account be taken out during each succeeding year. So no matter how high the rate of return, the account will wind down over time, particularly after age 80.

TABLE 6.4: Investment Scenarios for Jack's LIF

Assumptions: Male age 62 and an initial account value of $500,000

Age	3% Returns		5% Return		7% Return	
	Monthly Income	Jan. 1 Value	Monthly Income	Jan. 1 Value	Monthly Income	Jan. 1 Value
62	$2,460	$500,000	$2,460	$500,000	$2,460	$500,000
65	$2,411	$441,164	$2,561	$468,527	$2,584	$497,016
68	$2,283	$403,607	$2,531	$434,679	$2,848	$489,069
70	$2,132	$349,637	$2,503	$410,452	$2,930	$480,366
73	$2,086	$297,757	$2,601	$371,291	$3,230	$461,029
77	$1,977	$264,382	$2,472	$313,293	$3,325	$421,122
80	$1,676	$183,732	$2,409	$264,066	$3,439	$376,887
85	$1,328	$107,234	$2,117	$170,955	$3,218	$270,097
90	$736	$45,620	$1,263	$80,981	$2,218	$142,157
95	$294	$17,670	$582	$34,966	$1,137	$68,277
100	$114	$6,844	$251	$15,097	$546	$32,793

Because one of the factors in determining the maximum amount that can be paid from a LIF is the value of your account on January 1 of each year, there is going to be some variance in the amount of your LIF income from year to year. This variance may be significant if you have your LIF invested in a variable portfolio. All you need to do is look back at January 1, 2009, to get a sense of how the portfolio's value might affect your income. Projections for LIF income amounts, including the ones used in this book, assume an average rate of return. That means if I assume 5 per cent as the average rate, the projections apply 5 per cent each and every year. Obviously, with variable portfolios that is not going to be how the returns are realized in actuality.

Commuting Your Pension

As stated previously, if you have reasonable tenure in a pension program, choosing what to do with that asset may be the biggest financial decision you ever have to make. One of the biggest aspects of this decision is whether or not to commute your pension value and move it to a LIRA or locked-in RRSP instead of electing a formal pension income. While commuting your pension gives you much more flexibility and additional planning options, it also exposes you to some uncertainties that otherwise would have been addressed by the formal pension annuity.

There are always other considerations that come into play; it is not simply a case of comparing incomes or estate values from each option. So when I discuss this decision with clients, I want to make sure I understand their rationale for wanting to commute their pension. It is also important for them to have answers to the following questions. If this is a decision you are making, then you need to think through and/or find answers to these as well.

- What are the reasons that commuting your pension appeals to you?
- What are the survivor/estate entitlements under the pension income options?
- Is there a bridging benefit that you would lose?
- What is the rate of return a LIF/LRIF would have to realize in order to match the pension income?
- Do you understand the income-splitting rules regarding formal pension income vs. LIF income before age 65?
- Do you forgo extended health benefits or other pensioner entitlements (e.g., life insurance) if you elect to commute?
- Is there any amount of your commuted value that cannot be tax sheltered? The Income Tax act limits the benefit amount that may be transferred on a tax-sheltered basis. This is known as the maximum transfer value (MTV). The portion of a benefit that exceeds this limit will be considered taxable as income.

The commuted value of your pension will be moved to a locked-in retirement account (LIRA) if it is provincially regulated or to a locked-in RRSP if federally regulated.

Unlocking Locked-In Funds

As you have read, there are restrictions on how and how much income can be removed. Many people with locked-in accounts resent the limitations that are imposed on this type of asset. But there are ways to "free up" amounts of locked-in money in order to provide more flexibility to your assets and, ultimately, to provide you with more choices.

Depending on the jurisdiction governing your locked-in account, you may have the option to unlock a portion of your pension proceeds. By "unlock," I simply mean having the ability to transfer a portion of your locked-in money to your RRSP or an RRSP-like vehicle, thereby making it totally flexible for you to use. Federal as well as most provincial rules allow the owner of a locked-in account to unlock 50 per cent of the value of the account. This happens at the time the locked-in account is moved to a LIF, LRIF or RLIF. Saskatchewan permits 100 per cent unlocking after age 55 if certain requirements are met.

The rules and the timing of this provision vary among provinces and with federal legislation as well. These provisions show that both provincial and federal legislators recognize that it is appropriate to allow people to have some discretion with the retirement funds they have built up through a pension.

If you have a locked-in account but are not drawing from it for your retirement income, there is a way to free up amounts of money each year. As long as you have met the required age under the governing legislation, the following steps can help release some of the locked-in capital each year.

1. Convert your LIRA to a LIF or LRIF or your locked-in RRSP to an RLIF.
2. Begin taking income on a "minimum withdrawal" basis.
3. Transfer the difference between the minimum withdrawal and the maximum withdrawal amount to an RRSP.

The transfer of the amount between the LIF minimum and maximum withdrawal must go into an RRSP that is in the name of the LIF owner. This could be done right up to the age of 71. The transfer does not require or use any RRSP contribution room, as it is a direct transfer. However, the minimum amount must be brought into taxable income. If you have RRSP contribution room, you can turn that payment into a contribution to your own or to a spousal RRSP and negate the taxation of that payment. When you ultimately do require income from the LIF or LRIF, then the maximum income is simply paid out to you instead of your RRSP, so the transition is seamless.

Comparing the Life Annuity and LIF

This isn't so much about getting exactly what you want. Most of the time, as in the examples just presented, what you want does not exist. It is more about deciding what it is you are prepared to give up. If you want the guarantees of the annuity option, you are going to give up the flexibility that the LIF will provide. If you want the flexibility of the LIF, you are going to give up the guarantees that come with the annuity.

The Income that Can Be Generated

The first point of comparison is the amount of income that can be withdrawn from a LIF and the income offered by the pension plan (annuity). Often, the pension plan will provide a higher initial income, especially for a single life annuity. A single life annuity for Jack, guaranteed for 10 years (pension option 2), paid $2,643 monthly. It is important to remember that the pension plan income is an annuity which, by design, is a principal encroachment vehicle. This becomes evident when you compare the asset/estate value of the different options as shown in the next comparison.

The pension option Jack favoured (option 9) delivered a guaranteed monthly income of $2,259 for as long as either he or Diane were living. As you can see from Table 6.4, the LIF for Jack would pay an initial monthly income of $2,460. The amount of income provided by the LIF at a 5 per cent investment return exceeds the amount of pension income until age 80, at which time it starts to decline. The pension income, although lower initially, never declines. And, to state the obvious, if the LIF returns are in the 7 per cent range, the income keeps pace with the pension to age 90. Similarly, lower returns would lower the LIF income to well below the level of the pension payments.

Also, as you will recall, formal pension income (the annuity) qualifies for pension splitting and as eligible income for pension credit at any age.

That is a benefit not afforded the LIF income until Jack reaches the age of 65. And Diane would have to wait until she turned 65 to use any of the split LIF income for her pension credit.

The Estate Value

The estate value from the pension annuity is provided in the form of the guarantee period. With Jack's pension, he was looking at the option that provided a 15-year guarantee. Since this is a joint annuity, if either he or Diane has received 180 monthly payments, the guarantee period is finished. If they both drove off of a cliff 15 years and one month after the pension had commenced and they perished, there would be no value to the estate.

The estate value from the LIF is simply the balance in the account. There is no opportunity to set up the LIF on a joint life basis. It can only be in Jack's name since he is the pension plan member, but Diane would be named as the beneficiary. If Jack passed away, the account would transfer title to Diane and would be considered a tax-free rollover. As the named beneficiary, she would also have the option of transferring the balance to her own RRSP/RRIF account and in so doing would remove the locked-in status and restrictions. If Diane pre-deceased Jack, another beneficiary could be named. Unless it is a spouse, however, the proceeds would be fully taxable to the estate at Jack's subsequent passing. Not that I'm rushing Jack into getting remarried! And herein is a very important point about why you need to be careful with any beneficiary designations for registered accounts where it is a person other than a spouse. The named beneficiary will receive the proceeds of the account, but your estate will be responsible for the tax bill. That could create some real complications for those who are named in the will as beneficiaries of your estate.

Here is a comparative estimate of how the estate values break down, using the numbers from the LIF with a 5 per cent return compared to the joint life annuity guaranteed for 15 years. Figures are shown for the values at the end of each year.

TABLE 6.5: Estate Value of LIF versus Annuity

Age	Annuity	LIF	Age	Annuity	LIF
62	$401,305	$489,971	70	$227,090	$397,799
63	$378,120	$479,380	71	$200,035	$384,725
64	$360,123	$468,527	72	$171,360	$371,291
65	$341,055	$457,440	73	$140,960	$357,567
66	$320,840	$446,148	74	$108,730	$343,252
67	$299,410	$434,679	75	$74,580	$328,459
68	$276,695	$422,614	76	$38,375	$313,293
69	$252,615	$410,452	77	$0	$297,546

The estate values in the LIF account are higher for two reasons. First, as mentioned earlier, the annuity is a principal-encroachment vehicle by design, so it uses up capital to create the income payment. Second, I am comparing the annuity to a 5 per cent return on the LIF. This projected rate of return is higher than current bond rates, which is what would be used in the calculation of the pension annuity.

The Unique Features of Each Option
Pension Annuity
- guaranteed income for life
- no ongoing investment decisions required
- not affected by stock market or interest rate changes
- formal pension payments are eligible pension income
- does not allow for inflation adjustments (other than public sector plans)
- inflexible contract once purchased
- joint annuitant cannot be changed
- income cannot be stopped
- not as likely to provide a benefit to the estate

LIF and LRIF
- automatically single life; no option for joint
- ongoing investment decisions required
- potentially higher or lower income than annuity

- you control income flow within limits
- can be rolled back to a LIRA or locked-in RRSP if under age 71
- spousal beneficiary able to remove "locked-in" restriction
- eligible as pension income after age 65
- more likely to provide a benefit to estate
- can be partially or fully converted to an annuity at any age

I am not trying to make a case here for one option or the other. These vehicles are different and they have different features. But it is because of the very flexible nature of the LIF that it attracts a great deal of attention as an option.

Severance Packages

In recognition of long-term employment and service to the organization, a severance package may be offered when an employee departs. How do you most efficiently deal with your severance package? Normally these are large sums, which, if simply added as fully-taxable income on top of normal income or salary, can result in a substantial amount of tax payable. However, there may be options that serve to defer, reduce or eliminate the tax bill and preserve more of the severance for you. These options include the following and should be considered in the order that they appear.

Rollover Provisions

You may be able to roll over some or all of the severance into your RRSP, within certain limits. Under a special provision known as a "retiring allowance," you are permitted to transfer $2,000 for each year of service up to the end of 1995, plus an additional $1,500 per year prior to 1989 if you were not a member of a pension plan or if benefits under the pension plan were not vested. No credit for the purpose of calculating transfer limits is given for years after 1995. This does not require or involve any RRSP contribution room. You cannot move this money into a spousal RRSP plan, nor can you make use of your spouse's RRSP contribution room.

Unused RRSP Contribution Room

If you have unused RRSP contribution room (including the current year's contribution), this should be the next step. A direct transfer and "tax adjustment at source" can be requested so that pre-tax dollars are used to make the contribution. This adjustment of source would allow payment directly to your RRSP account without all of the usual deductions (including income tax) that would otherwise have to be made before payment. This simply means more money into your RRSP account sooner. This contribution can go either to your RRSP or a spousal RRSP account using your own personal contribution room. (Be careful, though, about income attribution rules pertaining to spousal RRSPs if withdrawals are planned within three calendar years.)

These first two options allow for pre-tax amounts to be used, as tax is not withheld at source.

Remaining Cash Payments

If you have used the above options to shelter as much of the payment as possible, or you are not eligible for either of the options above, you'll now have to bring the rest of the severance into taxable income. With the after-tax money in your possession, you should consider:

- topping-up your spouse's RRSP, if he or she has contribution room
- reducing non-deductible debt

Defer Payment of Severance

You can request that your employer pay out the severance over more than the current calendar year. This does not have much benefit if you are going to seek employment at an income level similar to what you were earning. In that case, you are normally better off to take the payment, shelter what you can, pay the tax on the balance and then have use of the capital sooner rather than later. If, however, you are close to retirement and your income level may change meaningfully over the next couple of years, this approach may have merit.

Tax-Preferred Investments (e.g., Flow-through Shares)

Certain investments carry a tax credit/deduction enhancement, and these may be worth investigating in certain cases. Remember that the tax benefits are a trade-off for greater investment risk, and you should make sure that you are fully aware of what those risk issues could be.

Lastly, you may have accumulated unused sick days. In lieu of being paid out for these in the form of taxable income, you can have the value transferred directly to your personal RRSP, if you have retiring allowance room. Accrued vacation cannot be transferred in any form, not even as a retiring allowance. Any benefit from this source must be taken as a taxable receipt. You could also, at the discretion of the employer, simply extend the formal retirement date by the number of days of vacation and be paid for that period, also potentially retaining your benefits during that time.

Deferred Profit Sharing Plans

You may participate in a deferred profit sharing plan (DPSP) in addition to or instead of a pension plan. These plans allow employers to make, within limits, tax-deductible, tax-deferred contributions to an employee's account. There are many reasons why employers who wish to contribute to an employee's retirement account would choose to use this vehicle. One of the key features for the employer is that, with the exception of an annual minimum, there is no fixed amount of contribution as there is with a regular pension plan. As a participant in the plan, you should be aware of this. There will likely be varying amounts of contributions to your account, depending on the profitability of the company.

A DPSP cannot accept employee contributions, except for transfers from other tax-assisted plans. Full employee vesting (entitlement to the contributions) occurs after 24 months of DPSP membership. Unlike a formal pension plan, locking-in rules do not apply to these accounts, and you have total flexibility and portability upon termination or retirement (if vested).

From the perspective of planning, flexibility is good. The fact that DPSP values can be moved to an RRSP and treated accordingly is a real advantage to these programs. If you participate in a DPSP and terminate or retire from the employer, the most practical alternative is to roll the account balance into a personally held RRSP.

MAKING YOUR BLUEPRINT WORK FOR YOU

1. Many retirees choose to work and, therefore, earn income from employment. A dollar of income from employment is one that does not have to come from personal assets and, as such, serves to help conserve your income-producing assets. There are also the added social benefits of the workplace. And there is a big difference between working because you want to and working because you have to. Going forward, I suspect we will all see that many retiring Baby Boomers will have work, in some manner, form part of their sustainable retirement lifestyle.

2. What to do with your pension account is the biggest financial decision you will ever make. You only get one opportunity to decide what to do with this asset. So that should only be done with all of the information at hand. Make sure you know what type of pension you have (defined benefit or defined contribution) and any extra options that are available to you (such as indexing).

3. One option for creating income from your pension is a life annuity, which offers a guaranteed stream of income for life. However, interest rates are currently at 50-year lows. This does not necessarily make it a great time to buy a life annuity that will lock in those rates for the next 30 years. But if you are looking for guaranteed income and want pension-splitting opportunities under the age of 65, a formal annuity income from the pension will allow you to do this. If there is meaningful longevity in your family history, an annuity is a valid consideration.

4. The second option for creating income from your pension is a Life Income Fund, which does not offer guaranteed income but does provide more flexibility than an annuity. If your family history is not one of long life then you may find the LIF a better choice. Certainly in a situation where the health and longevity of the pensioner are questionable, the use of a LIF will provide needed flexibility for survivors and the estate. Remember that if you commute your pension you can elect to have some of the proceeds in a LIF and use some to purchase a life annuity. This provides the proverbial "best of both worlds." Keep in mind, though, that done in this manner, the annuity payment will not qualify as eligible income for either the pension credit or income splitting until the annuitant is age 65.

5. When you are considering what to do with a severance payment, follow the steps I have laid out in this chapter. These sums need to be handled in the most tax-efficient manner possible in order for you to realize the greatest benefit.

6. Think of the benefits that you may have accrued in your Deferred Profit Sharing Plan (DPSP) like an RRSP account. The options you have for drawing out DPSP money are similar to those available to RRSPs. In fact, the most common option chosen by those taking money from their DPSP account is to actually roll it directly into their RRSP.

7

PERSONAL SOURCES OF INCOME

Taxable Distributions from Non-Registered Assets

So far we have layered income starting with government benefits and income from pensions or locked-in accounts. I have already stated that it is most beneficial to use non-registered (tax-paid) assets when you move into the higher tax brackets. So why are we talking about using non-registered income before we even get to RRSPs?

What I am referring to here is not the use of your non-registered assets in a planned and structured way, but that of the dividends, interest and realized capital gains distributed from your investments, which are all taxable in the year they are paid to you.

I often see situations where people in retirement have non-registered mutual funds and the taxable distributions are being reinvested. They own GICs, and the interest is compounding in the certificate. Don't do that! During the income phase, any interest, dividends or capital gains that are distributed from non-registered GICs, GIAs, bonds, mutual funds et cetera should be paid out to you as income rather than compounded or reinvested. Compounding your GIC is simply compounding your tax problem. Have the interest paid out to you.

There are better and more effective ways to have more control over the taxable distributions from your non-registered investments, in terms of sheltering, control and actual tax treatment. I will look at several of these options in the Special Tools and Strategies section of this book. Shortly, I will also be discussing the Tax-Free Savings Account (TFSA), which is one of the most useful tools to be introduced in years. It does a perfect job, within the contribution limits allowed, of negating taxation on the earnings and growth of the non-registered investments held within it.

RRSPs

Up to this point, we have dealt with income sources that are fully taxable and are either inflexible such as CPP and OAS or, in the case of pensions and locked-in accounts, have limitations on how income can be created. Now we are going to look at RRSPs as the next layer in building the cash flow you need. Granted, the payments from RRSP/RRIF plans are fully taxable, but you do have a greater degree of access to these accounts than you do with anything we have discussed to this point.

RRSPs are still one of the most effective tools for accumulating retirement assets. I encourage people to contribute as much as they can, to the maximum they are allowed, especially in the early years. There is a possibility of having government benefits reduced or clawed back if your net income in retirement is too high, so you may be wondering why I would still suggest maximizing RRSP contributions if the eventual withdrawals are fully taxable. The main answer is this: for people with higher levels of taxable income, the deduction resulting from an RRSP contribution is significant. Think of the tax savings that you realize as the government helping you to build your retirement nest egg. If you are in the second tax bracket, you will be taxed at between 31 to 38 per cent on each dollar, depending on your province of residence. What this means in terms of your RRSP is that it takes only $0.62 to $0.69 of your take-home pay to make a $1.00 contribution. In addition, the growth in your account is tax sheltered and deferred. It is only when you start to take money out that it becomes taxable. To be able to deduct and defer makes the whole concept appealing from both a taxation and accumulation perspective.

But in order to make your RRSP work effectively for you, there are two key planning issues that need to be addressed in your blueprint.

First, much like contributing to a money purchase (defined contribution) pension plan, you know what you are putting into your RRSPs. But do you know what it will mean when you retire? What level of sustainable income will your RRSP account create for you? More importantly, what level of after-tax income will your RRSPs be able to generate? Most people I meet for the first time have absolutely no idea of the answers to these questions. Yes, you may have built up a very large account value in your RRSP, but remember that this has to produce income for you over the next 25 to 35 years.

Second, you need to have an exit strategy for these assets. You need to have both a short-term and long-term approach to how your registered accounts will be used. Remember, your RRSPs are one of the most flexible assets you have at your disposal. Your blueprint needs to map out how they will complement and layer with your other sources of income. It also should detail how your RRSP will work with the intelligent disassembly strategy for your assets.

Spousal RRSPs

The four Ds of effective tax planning are: deduct, divide, defer and discount. Spousal RRSPs incorporate the first three of these strategies. You and your spouse are permitted, within your respective contribution limits, to structure the ownership of your RRSPs in any manner you choose. As is the case with other assets, RRSP accounts cannot be transferred from one individual to another, with the exception of at divorce or death. So ownership of the RRSP account must be established at the time the contribution is made.

The objective in splitting assets is to create two streams of income in retirement. This is more effective than having the majority of income in the name of only one taxpayer. Each individual has their own set of exemptions, tax credits and graduated personal rates. The end result is the same flow of total income for the household but greater after-tax income. With the introduction of the pension splitting rules, one might ask if there is still relevance in balancing the accumulations for RRSPs. The answer is yes. Remember that the income splitting rules for RRSP accounts will only take effect at age 65 and beyond, and only when income is created from a RRIF.

So, there still is merit in having some balance as these assets are being accumulated in case you start your income before age 65.

In terms of planning withdrawals from spousal RRSPs, keep in mind something that is referred to as the "three-year rule." If withdrawals are made from a spousal RRSP within the three calendar years preceding the last contribution, the amount withdrawn will be added to the taxable income of the contributor. There is a relationship between the amount of withdrawal and the amount of the last contribution, but I won't get into detail here. The simple rule to follow to avoid any problems is this: have two full calendar years between the time of the last spousal contribution and the first withdrawal from a spousal account.

People are often of the erroneous belief that if a spousal contribution was made 10 years ago, it is permissible to collapse that one account or certificate and not have the three-year rule apply. This is not correct. The government views *any* spousal RRSP withdrawal within the three years preceding the last contribution as attributable to you, regardless of the timing of any individual placements. After the two full calendar years have elapsed, the spouse can remove whatever amount of income he or she wishes, and it will be taxed in his or her hands.

Income Options for Your RRSP

You are able to draw capital from your RRSPs at any time simply by making lump-sum withdrawals from the account. But to create a regular stream of income, you will need to convert your RRSP into one of three options—a life annuity, an annuity certain or a RRIF. You can elect any one of them or any combination of them. You are free to do this at any time, but the latest this move can be deferred to is December 31 of the year in which you turn 71. At that time, your RRSP is deemed to have matured. You must decide before that time what you are going to do with the assets.

1. Life Annuity (Single or Joint)

These are described in detail in Chapter 6. As a reminder, an annuity is an income delivery vehicle where the annuitant receives a guaranteed payment, made up of both principal and interest, in exchange for the proceeds of the account. There is no capital balance as the income is purchased with the amount of the RRSP proceeds used for this option.

The payments are guaranteed to be paid for life and do not change with fluctuations in markets or interest rates. Life annuities from RRSP proceeds can be indexed on a fixed basis of 1 to 4 per cent per year. While this does provide for some inflation protection, the initial income is lower than that delivered by a non-indexed life annuity.

2. Annuity Certain to Age 90

Like the above option, this form of annuity is a form of income purchased with RRSP capital. It pays a constant amount of monthly income until you turn 90. If death should occur before age 90, the balance of remaining payments would be paid to your estate. It is the only form of term-certain annuity permitted for RRSP funds. Mechanically, it would be possible to structure a RRIF to accomplish the same thing without the rigid structure of an annuity, but the RRIF would not provide the guaranteed income found in this type of annuity.

3. Registered Retirement Income Fund (RRIF)

By far, a RRIF is the most common and practical option for delivering income from RRSP accumulations. Since nearly all RRSPs being converted to an income vehicle are moved to a RRIF, this will be the focus of this section on using RRSP money in retirement.

RRIFs

There are several well-deserved reasons for the popularity of the RRIF as a vehicle to deliver income from RRSP proceeds, including:

- a variety of income options
- an ability to change income amounts
- an ability to make lump-sum withdrawals

- much greater flexibility than an annuity
- account balances that transfer to a surviving spouse without taxation
- potential for the account balance to become part of the estate
- smooth transition from RRSPs

When acquiring an annuity with RRSP proceeds, your holdings or investments are sold and the capital is used to purchase the annuity. When creating a RRIF account, existing RRSP investments can remain the same if that is what you wish. Your existing RRSP investments just move "in kind" (as is) into your RRIF account Think of it like taking a number of cars and pulling them out of one garage called an RRSP and moving them into a new garage called a RRIF. The cars remain the same; they are just housed in a different building.

With RRIFs, ongoing investment decisions will be required, but they also provide a great deal of flexibility. There is no limit on how many RRIF contracts you can own. You may wish to employ a number of plans with different withdrawal options to meet specific objectives. For example, you may have a need for a RRIF plan that delivers a core stream of income for month-to-month cash flow. You also may wish to have a RRIF that provides an additional monthly amount for the four months of the year when you are spending the winter in Florida. Finally, you may want to see a specific deposit into a separate account to satisfy the quarterly instalments that you must pay to the tax department. You are also able to make lump-sum withdrawals from your RRIF in addition to your scheduled payments. That said, it is also worthwhile to remember that any portion of an RRSP can be used for this purpose, and all of your RRSPs need not be converted to a RRIF at one time.

In the Special Tools and Strategies section of this book, I will be looking in detail at a hybrid of annuities and traditional investments that can be used within a RRIF.

The Minimum Withdrawal Schedule

As mentioned, you have great flexibility in determining the amount of withdrawals you wish to make from your RRIF. Once the RRIF is established, however, there is a minimum income that must be withdrawn from it each year. This is a requirement regardless of your age at the time you move your RRSP to a RRIF. There is no required withdrawal in the calendar year that the RRIF contract is established, but this is how the minimum withdrawal formula works for each calendar year thereafter. If the RRIF owner is under the age of 71, the formula for minimum withdrawal is as follows: 1 / (90 – age on January 1) X Account Value. For example, if you own a RRIF and on January 1 of the following year you are 65, here is how the formula is applied. First, 90 – 65 = 25. Then 1/25 = 0.04 or 4 per cent. So 4 per cent of whatever your RRIF account value is on that same January 1 must be withdrawn and brought into your taxable income during that year. The "account value" is defined as the balance in the RRIF at January 1 of each year after the RRIF is created.

For age 71 and beyond, the minimum withdrawal formula is based on your age and the corresponding percentage of the value of your RRIF account on January 1 each year.

TABLE 7.1: RRIF Minimum Withdrawal Percentages

Age	%	Age	%	Age	%
70	5.00	78	8.33	86	10.79
71	7.38	79	8.53	87	11.33
72	7.48	80	8.75	88	11.96
73	7.59	81	8.99	89	12.71
74	7.71	82	9.27	90	13.62
75	7.85	83	9.58	91	14.73
76	7.99	84	9.93	92	16.12
77	8.15	85	10.33	93	19.92

Note: For RRIFs issued prior to 1993 (qualified plans), there is a different minimum withdrawal schedule that is lower initially but the same as the current schedule from age 78 onward. I have chosen to only illustrate the schedule for those RRIF contracts that came into existence after 1992.

There is a noticeable jump in the minimum income that must be removed between age 70 and 71. That increase from 5 to 7.38 per cent represents a substantial increase in taxable income from one year to the next. That is why deferring income from your registered accounts can create some problems in terms of the levels of taxable income that you must withdraw.

The minimum withdrawal calculation may be based on the age of the plan holder or the age of the spouse. If the objective is to remove as little income as possible, then the date of birth of the younger spouse should be used. The decision of whose age to use for the minimum withdrawal formula is made when the RRIF contract is created. The minimum withdrawal schedule for RRIFs is the very same schedule that applies to LIFs, LRIFs, RLIFs and PRIFs. Keep in mind that once the income commences from one of these vehicles, the minimum must be paid out each year. You do have the option, should you wish to stop income from your RRIF, to change it back to an RRSP, which does not have mandated withdrawals. This can be done as long as the minimum has been paid out for the calendar year and you are under the age of 71.

The Benefits of Consolidating Your RRIF Assets in a Self-Directed Account

Very early in the book, I outlined the importance of consolidating all of your income-generating assets with one advisor. For similar reasons, one of the best tools for consolidating registered holdings is a self-directed account. Occasionally, the term "self-directed" makes people worry that they are going to be responsible for all the decisions regarding their plan, including making the actual investments. This is an option, but quite often this type of vehicle is used in conjunction with an advisor, and the majority of direction comes from the advisor working with you. A self-directed plan allows you to pull together, under one umbrella, stocks, GICs, bonds, ETFs and other investments that you have scattered about in various institutions. Keep in mind that each type of registered account—RRSP, RRIF, LIRA, LIF and LRIF—requires its own self-directed plan, as these monies cannot be mixed together. As you move toward a target retirement date, a self-directed plan allows you to begin pulling together all of your registered accounts. These accounts may be held at different institutions and only be available for transfer at different times. A self-directed plan allows you to consolidate your holdings over time.

One of the additional benefits is that all activity in your self-directed account, including deposits, income payments, purchases, redemptions, changes to investments, interest and dividend payments, are recorded and summarized on your investment statement. This provides you with a detailed consolidated statement for all of your holdings within the plan.

Self-directed plans also have a role in terms of timing the sale of assets to provide income. For example, your RRIF may hold GICs among the different types of investments within it. You may not immediately be able to access them for income because they have maturity dates that are in the future. In a similar sense, you may have mutual funds that have a form of back-end load. You may not want to use those particular funds right away because of the potential charges. The self-directed RRIF will allow you to create the income stream you want from specific assets within the account. In this way, you can wait for GICs to mature or mutual fund sales charges to expire. Chapter 4 looks at another of the advantages provided by a self-directed plan, which is the ability to create income through the Cash Wedge strategy.

If you have several RRIFs scattered at different institutions, you must commence income from each one of these by the time you turn 71. With a self-directed plan, the flow of income, even if it is a minimum withdrawal, only has to come from one source. This means only one cheque, not several. The same holds true for mutual fund investments. If RRIFs are established with four different companies, that means four different deposits. If the same companies and investments are instead housed in a self-directed plan, then only one deposit is made to your bank account. Previously we looked at the concept of consolidating assets. Simplification, less administration and fewer cheques are some of the benefits of this course of action.

Topping Up to Bracket

If, up to this point, your taxable income from all other sources is not up to the top of the first federal tax bracket after pension splitting, then consideration should be given to drawing additional RRSP or RRIF amounts to get to that level. Even if this withdrawal is not needed for regular income, it is usually better to take out fully-taxable income at a lower bracket and convert the excess income to non-registered savings than to defer it and have it come out later at a higher tax rate. Let's look at an approach that can create greater efficiency for you both in the short term and the long term. I refer to it as "Topping Up to Bracket."

It may be disadvantageous to defer registered assets as long as possible for the purpose of "tax-sheltering." The following strategy may seem to be contrary to common planning practices, but it may be of great value in helping you to systematically disassemble your RRSPs and RRIFs and in avoiding the consequences of having too much registered money in later life.

The prolonged deferral of RRSP and other registered money can possibly lead you into a tax trap as you progress into your late 60s and beyond. It can also increase such costs as long-term care assessments and the taxes on estate values at death. Where there are larger accumulations of registered money, the concept of topping up to bracket is worthy of consideration.

The concept involves taking out additional taxable income even though it is not needed to meet cash flow requirements. It could simply be an additional sum that you withdraw, say to fund contributions to a Tax-Free Savings Account (TFSA). Or it could be to reach the top of the current tax bracket you find yourself in. It would fit into situations where you are most likely to be in the same tax bracket, and consequently at the same marginal tax rate, in the future. The prime consideration here is that within a specific tax bracket you are going to pay the same marginal rate on each dollar. Let's use an example.

Bob has just retired at age 60. His pension income from his defined benefit plan plus his CPP retirement benefit provides him with an annual income of $46,000. In 2011, he is in the second federal tax bracket. In fact, he will never be in a lower tax bracket from this point forward. So, any additional taxable income he receives will be taxed at the same marginal rate up to $83,088 (using 2011 federal brackets).

Bob will also have another (approximately) $6,000 of income a year from his OAS entitlement starting at age 65. If Bob defers his RRSP until his late sixties or early seventies, he may run the risk of having taxable and net income that is high enough to totally eliminate the Age Credit and reduce his OAS benefit. That is a form of needless double taxation.

An effective strategy for Bob, if he has large sums of RRSP money, may be to look at taking some of this RRSP money into income, even if it is not required for his regular cash flow. This strategy is particularly effective when done in the years before age 65, so that you don't erode the Age Credit or any OAS benefit.

What you are really doing is taking out additional income, paying the tax and converting it into non-registered money. There are investment vehicles available that will allow you to effectively defer taxation on your non-registered accounts while at the same time delivering tax-effective income. We will be going into detail about these tax-efficient options in Part Five. This strategy is consistent with the process of layering income in a tax-efficient manner and in line with the objectives of the Income Continuum.

It is also important for married couples to remember that one of them will probably pre-decease the other at some point. RRSP/RRIF accounts can transfer without taxation to the surviving spouse. But, a larger RRSP/RRIF value could dramatically increase the minimum withdrawal amount for the survivor. Once again, this could elevate net income levels to the point where benefits and entitlements are either reduced or eliminated.

A few years ago, I was creating training material on retirement income planning for one of the large Canadian financial institutions, and this concept was part of that content. One of the key people in charge of training asked me for clarification on the mechanics and merits of this approach because it is so contrary to what "old-school thinking" advocates. I went through the points listed here and then I got to "more survivor friendly." I explained that if you had two people in retirement who had divided their RRSP (and now RRIF) savings perfectly and who also had identical income streams, things would work very well until one of them passed away. Then, the balance of the deceased's RRSP account would roll over to the survivor. This would result in basically doubling the value of the survivor's RRIF. It would also double the amount of income that had to be removed as a minimum and could very well move that income into higher brackets and reduce Old Age Security payments. There was a pause as she looked at me and then she said, "Wow, you have just described the situation my mother-in-law finds herself in since her husband passed away." And that is the point. Where it is an appropriate strategy, bringing in additional amounts of fully-taxable income from RRIF accounts earlier and converting it to non-registered assets can make the delivery of future income more efficient, for you, your survivor and your estate.

Convert Your RRSP/RRIF and Defer Non-Registered Assets

The topping up to bracket strategy involves taking money out of a tax-sheltered vehicle, paying the tax and investing the tax-paid capital in an efficient manner. The section of this book that discusses taxation focuses on preserving government benefits and tax credits, which is one reason to engage this strategy. There are additional reasons to systematically convert registered money and place the net proceeds in non-registered accounts:

- creates more tax-effective income in the future
- creates an account to access for lump-sum withdrawals
- provides more control for client (no minimum withdrawal as with an RRIF)
- may permit asset/income splitting
- long-term care per diems may be lower if net income is lower
- more tax-efficient for spousal beneficiary
- more estate-friendly
    - taxation of the estate
    - potential assets for testamentary trusts

Discuss this with your advisor to see if it has merit for you. Basically, what you are trying to do is avoid a situation where the required RRIF withdrawals create net income levels where benefits are being lost. So there are many variables, including other sources of income. If your RRSP accounts are large and will continue to grow even after withdrawals for regular income, this strategy may apply. If your RRSP accounts will require you to take larger amounts of income out in future years, then this course of action may be beneficial. If it appears that by deferring the use of your RRSP accounts you may migrate into a higher tax bracket when your income starts, you should investigate this. However, if throughout your retirement, planned withdrawals from fully-taxable accounts, including government benefits, will have you comfortably below the limit of the first federal tax bracket, there may not be a need to consider this option. When considering how to create your income, it is important to consider how decisions you make today will impact how income is created in the future. That is the core principle of the Income Continuum.

Non-Registered Accounts

As you know by now, the effective layering of income requires that you use the least tax-efficient, least flexible sources of income first. Once that fully-taxable base of income has been established, then look to use more tax-efficient and non-taxable sources of income as you get into higher tax brackets. This is where and how non-registered assets are best used. I did include taxable distributions from non-registered investments as a layer of income, but what about using the actual after-tax capital? The vast majority of the tax-effective and creative income strategies available involve using non-registered assets. You will see this as we move into Part Five, which examines special tools and strategies. And it is in that section of the book that I will examine the use of non-registered assets within the layering process in more detail.

It is common to see little in the way of non-registered holdings in the assets of those about to retire. There are several reasons for this. Given the advantage of being able to deduct an RRSP contribution, this tends to be where most people put their retirement savings. In fact, I would contend that most individuals view the tax saving as the primary reason to make an RRSP contribution, with the objective of accumulating retirement assets being only secondary. Very few people actually make the maximum RRSP contributions to which they are entitled. As few as 35 per cent of all eligible taxpayers make any RRSP contribution at all. So, if non-registered savings occur after RRSPs are maximized, is it any wonder these amounts are usually small? That is one of the reasons that I try to help retirees create some non-registered assets through systematically converting their fully-taxable accounts as described earlier.

The Tax-Free Savings Account (TFSA)

Introduced in 2009, these plans are available for all individuals aged 18 and over who have a valid Social Insurance Number. The concept is to have an account where after-tax capital does not attract tax on investment returns at any point in the future. Contributions are non-deductible and, of course, are made with after-tax money. There are three key features to these plans:

1. contributions are not based on income
2. cumulative unused contribution room can be carried forward indefinitely
3. very flexible "in-out" provisions—any withdrawals restore contribution room

For 2009, 2010 and 2011, the contribution limit is $5,000 per person. The contribution room will be indexed in increments of $500 when warranted by increases in the CPI.

Additional Tax-Efficient Features

- Contributions may be made to a spouse's TFSA without attribution to the contributor. Income from these accounts will not factor into means testing for government entitlements.
- Withdrawals from this source will assist in income and asset splitting by helping to keep taxable income low. This in turn helps to preserve government benefits and tax credits.
- They are very useful in the topping up to bracket strategy or for investing CPP receipts. They have a very meaningful role to play in the intelligent disassembly of retirement assets.
- At the passing of a plan holder, the balance can transfer without tax to the surviving spouse and, in turn, at the death of the surviving spouse, can transfer to the estate tax free.

Being allowed only $5,000 per year in contributions may make this seem an insignificant tool in long-term planning. But over 20 or 30 years, that amount may allow for some significant account balances to accrue. That will allow them to serve as an extremely effective source of income and access to capital. The TFSA accounts will also be an excellent and efficient source from which to draw premiums for life and health insurance.

The fact that it is called a "savings account" does cause a bit of confusion. The name is appropriate because, like most other savings accounts, money can be moved in and out without sacrificing the contribution room (which happens when you withdraw from an RRSP account). However, the name suggests that the only investment for these vehicles is an actual savings account. So people have looked at me and asked why they would put money into a savings account that earns them little to no interest even if the amounts are earned tax free. In actual fact, the TFSA can be invested in the same way as your RRSP account or any other non-registered investment.

I firmly believe that moving forward, as account values build, the TFSA will become one of the great tools at our disposal. I look for ways to help retirees fund their TFSA accounts to the maximum, whether that be through taking CPP early, withdrawing additional amounts out of registered accounts or even moving other non-registered holdings systematically into them.

It is my opinion that you should do what you can to fund your TFSA every year. And I am not saying that you must contribute the maximum. This vehicle will become a very significant asset over time. If you can fund contributions from your cash flow, that is great. If not, you may have existing, non-registered assets from which you can transition an amount to your TFSA year after year. And my preference, as previously stated, is to unwind your fully-taxable assets to fund the TFSA contributions. This works effectively on so many levels.

Home Equity as a Source of Retirement Income

There are a number of ways that the equity you build in your principal residence can serve to either create an income stream or provide access to an amount of capital. In either option, the receipts are free from taxation. You are not taxed when you take out a loan, and that's really what you are doing, whether in the form of a reverse mortgage or a line of credit against the equity of your home. In either option, the idea is to be able to access some of the value of the equity in your property while still living there. After all, you can't sell part of your house. The issue here is that you will then either have to service loan interest or run the risk of having a larger and larger amount of interest capitalizing and reducing the value of this asset when it is sold or it transfers to your estate.

It is a respectable objective to wish to remain in your own home. But that in turn is going to mean maintenance costs that could become higher as your home becomes older. And there may very well come a time when you either want to or have to move. Remember that while you may not be required to repay what has been borrowed while you live in the home, that payment will be due if you sell your home. What will you be left with after the proceeds of the sale are reduced by what you must pay back? And how will those reduced proceeds affect your options in terms of where you will live next? Obviously this would also affect the value of the estate if your home was sold after your death.

The decision to tap into the equity of your home should not be made lightly. In my opinion, this step should be taken only after other income-generating avenues have been explored, and then only as an action that is necessary to provide additional cash flow. You should also seek independent legal counsel and actively discuss this decision with other family members. The earliest age at which someone can entertain this strategy is 62, according to the institutions who provide the loans. I would certainly suggest that you wait until you are in your early seventies before considering this. That is why it is listed as the very last source of potential income. Investigate your options and compare the reverse mortgage and line of credit offerings before making any final decisions.

MAKING YOUR BLUEPRINT WORK FOR YOU

1. At the time you retire, have any taxable distributions from your non-registered investments, be they mutual funds, stocks, bonds, ETFs or GICs, paid out to you as income. Do not have them reinvested. If you are using GICs, do not have the interest compounding. You will be taxed on these on an annual basis. Let the cash flow created from these also help you pay the income tax that you will have to pay on these receipts.

2. RRSPs are still one of the best retirement accumulation tools you can use. But you need to have an "exit strategy" for them in terms of how they will be used to most efficiently create income for you over the time you are retired.

3. Look for efficient ways to defer non-registered assets rather than your registered accounts. There is a whole process of conversion that will need to take place over the time you are retired. Do you have this mapped out in a blueprint?

4. Tax-Free Savings Accounts (TFSAs) will become one of the most useful and significant financial tools you will have at your disposal over the next number of years. This vehicle is the first choice when it comes to systematically converting any RRSP/RRIF withdrawals that are not required to create your regular retirement income.

5. Tapping into home equity as a source of retirement income is an option. But in my opinion, for most people it is an option that should be a last consideration. It should also not be a course of action until you are at least in your early seventies and after basically all other alternatives have been explored. Do not base your retirement planning around this strategy.

PART
FOUR

ESSENTIAL TAX CONSIDERATIONS

8

IT'S FLOODIN' DOWN IN TAXES

Note: Valuable updates for this book, including tax figures and illustrations, are available at www.boomersblueprint.com.

Paying taxes on income is the one thing that is less fun than spending money on auto repairs. And for most Canadians, it is one of the biggest expenses in retirement. The tax laws are the rules you must adhere to when drafting your blueprint (sort of like being required to build to code). So while this may not be the most stimulating part of the book to read, it is very important that you have a comfortable understanding of the taxation issues that do and will affect you. This is an area where there is much waste and inefficiency, simply because people either have no blueprint or have one that has been poorly drafted.

This chapter will review what I have found to be the essential tax considerations in retirement income planning. While there are some basic points on taxation that need to be illustrated here, I don't want this to read like a text book. What I want to do is identify what I repeatedly see as the key taxation issues for retirement income. Then, in this and succeeding chapters, I will show you some of the tools at your disposal and the related strategies for using them, which will help you to reduce taxes on your retirement income now and in the future. Addressing these taxation issues is also the foundation for layering income, which I explore in more detail in Step 4 of the Six-Step Plan.

Taxing Your Income

The first thing to do is to quickly run through some definitions so that you understand the flow of taxation in arriving at net and taxable income. An image of the first page of the "Income Tax Estimator" will help you to visualize what I am describing.

FIGURE 8.1: Income Tax Estimator

Income Tax Estimator	Tax Year 2011 ▼

Identification

Province	Ontario ▼			Taxpayer	Spouse
Children	none ▼	☐ Single	Age	65 to 69 ▼	65 to 69 ▼

Total income

	Taxpayer	Spouse
Employment Income	$14,719.00	$0.00
Old Age Security pension	$6,310.00	$6,310.00
Eligible pension income	$32,616.00	$22,011.00
Employment insurance benefits	$0.00	$0.00
Canadian dividends (actual amount received from CCPC)	$0.00	$0.00
Canadian dividends (actual amount received from Public corp)	$0.00	$0.00
Dividend gross up	$0.00	$0.00
Other Ordinary Income: Interest, CPP, Foreign Pension, etc.	$7,875.00	$8,893.00
Capital gains (actual gain)	$0.00	$0.00
Non-taxable portion	$0.00	$0.00
Self-employment income (bus., prof., farm., fish.)	$0.00	$0.00
Total income	**$61,520.00**	**$37,214.00**

Net income

	Taxpayer	Spouse
RRSP deduction	$0.00	$0.00
Canada Pension Plan contributions on self employment earnings	$0.00	$0.00
Other deductions	$0.00	$0.00
Social benefit repayment (EI / OAS)	$0.00	$0.00
Net income	**$61,520.00**	**$37,214.00**

Taxable income

	Taxpayer	Spouse
Deductions from net income	$0.00	$0.00
Taxable income	**$61,520.00**	**$37,214.00**

Reprinted with courtesy and permission of www.walterharder.com

1. Your income from all sources is added up to arrive at your "Total Income."
2. After subtracting deductions, which include RRSP contributions, CPP contributions, deductible interest and others, you arrive at your "Net Income."
3. Your "Taxable Income" is calculated by subtracting other allowable deductions from your "Net Income" figure.

For the vast majority of retirees, the taxable income and net income numbers are the same amount.

The Federal Tax Brackets

Taxable income is the figure used in determining the amount of federal and provincial tax payable. After the basic personal exemption to which all taxpayers are entitled, there are four federal tax brackets. Canada has what is called a progressive tax system, which simply means that your rate of tax becomes higher as your taxable income increases. Based on the measure of taxable income for the year, the rate is applied and the amount of federal tax is calculated as shown below. Provinces and territories use the same income brackets but have their own rates and may also have additional intervening brackets. Table 8.2 below shows the federal rates as well as a comparative column that shows a sample of the combined federal/provincial rate for 2011.

TABLE 8.2: 2011 Personal Income Tax Rates

Bracket	Taxable Income	Federal Tax	Sample Combined Federal and Provincial Tax
	$0–$10,527	0%	0%
1st	$10,528–$41,544	15%	21%
2nd	$41,545–$83,088	22%	31%
3rd	$83,089–$128,800	26%	43%
4th	$128,801 and over	29%	46%

According to the Desjardins Rethink Retirement Survey 2009, 44 per cent of Canadian retirees had personal income under $30,000 and 49 per cent of them had incomes between $30,000 and $70,000. As such, I am going to focus most of my attention on the first two tax brackets (individual income up to $83,088 for 2011).

As you can see from the above table, there is no federal tax payable on what is referred to as "the personal amount," which is $10,527. The table also assumes that the personal exemption for the province used in the illustration is the same as it is for the federal personal exemption. This may be the case where you live, but most provinces and territories have their own personal amounts that are lower or higher than the number used federally.

You may have heard the terms "average tax rate" and "marginal tax rate," and it is important that you know what these mean and how they are different. Let's use an example of an individual taxpayer, age 63, who has $70,000 of taxable income in 2011. The first $10,527 of income is not taxed as that is the personal exemption amount. And I will assume that the provincial personal amount is identical.

The tax on her income between $10,528 and $41,544,
at 21 per cent, would be $6,513.

The tax on her income between $41,545 and $70,000,
at 31 per cent, would be $8,821.

Therefore, her total income tax payable on $70,000
is $15,334 ($6,513 + $8,821).

The "average tax rate" is the total tax owed as a percentage of total income. In the case above the average rate is (15,334 / 70,000 x 100) = 21.91 %. The "marginal tax rate" is that which is applied to the next dollar of taxable income. For the example above it would be 31 %, because her income finishes in the second bracket. The marginal tax rate is a significant consideration in tax planning since it represents the highest rate of tax you pay on your income at that level. Many of the strategies within this book are designed to reduce taxes by moving your income out of the higher tax brackets.

Lastly, tax brackets, exemptions, social benefit repayment thresholds and taxable income limits for determining credits are all indexed to the consumer price index (CPI) and adjusted yearly. Aside from helping Canadians deal with inflation, this is an important factor as it relates to deferring taxation into the future. It may mean lower inclusion rates and greater tax credits, which would result in a lower amount of tax payable.

Taxation on Different Forms of Income

It is likely that your various income sources in retirement will be treated differently for tax purposes. Your total income may come from many sources, some of which may be fully taxable, some may be tax favoured and some sources may not be taxable.

Fully-Taxable Income

For most retirees, the majority of income is drawn from sources that are fully taxable. The obvious income streams that fall under this tax treatment include, CPP benefits and OAS benefits as well as any employment income and rental income. Income that is derived from registered assets, such as pension payments, RRSP/RRIF payments and income drawn from locked-in accounts through a Life Income Fund (LIF), is fully taxable.

Investment Income from Non-Registered Assets

Normally, if money is invested outside of a sheltered vehicle such as an RRSP or a Tax-Free Savings Account (TFSA), the interest, dividends and realized capital gains from those investments (otherwise known as "taxable distributions") is taxable. These different types of distributions also receive different tax treatment, as described below.

Interest

Interest earned on non-registered investments is fully taxable. Furthermore, the interest earned must be declared and taxed annually, whether or not it was paid in cash (such as with compounding GICs or strip bonds). So GICs, bonds or bond funds, fixed income ETFs, mortgage funds and cash accounts distribute taxable interest on an annual basis. Some corporate class mutual funds (CCMFs) are an exception to this, and will be discussed in Chapter 10.

Dividends

Because dividends are paid out of after-tax corporate earnings, they are taxed in a different manner than interest. The dividend tax credit applies only to "eligible dividends," which are defined as those dividends paid from Canadian companies taxed at the general corporate rate. The amount of dividends you receive is first "grossed up" and that larger value is included in the net income calculation. Federal tax payable is then reduced by tax credit equal to a percentage of the grossed-up amount. This allows for an integration of personal and corporate taxes in flowing the income out of the corporation to the shareholders.

But the important consideration here is that the amount of the gross-up is included in the calculation of net income. So dividend income could be a disadvantage if you are trying to keep your net income figure low. In 2011, for example, $10,000 of eligible dividend income would have a gross-up of $4,100 and result in $14,100 being used in calculating total and net incomes. That increased income could serve to erode things like the age amount and OAS benefits or to even move the recipient into a higher tax bracket.

One of the reasons that dividend income *sounds* so appealing is that an individual can have just over $65,000 of (eligible) dividend income and pay no tax—but only if he or she had no other taxable income. Realistically, however, since dividend yields usually run around 3%, you would need about $2,000,000 of non-registered money invested in dividend-paying stocks to realize that level of dividend payout . . . and that is assuming that there are no management fees.

All dividends from Canadian corporations receive a dividend tax credit, although ineligible dividends have a lower gross-up and lower credit. Dividends earned from non-resident companies are taxed as regular income.

Capital gains and losses

When you sell something for more than you paid for it, you incur a capital gain. If the reverse happens, you incur a capital loss. With interest and dividend income, you are taxed in the year that these are earned or paid out to you. However, a capital gain only becomes taxable when it is realized. In many cases you have control of when this happens. And only

50 per cent of realized capital gains are included when determining income. If one of your goals with your non-registered holdings is to defer taxation, then investing for growth in the form of capital gains is an ideal strategy. Capital property consists of things such as property, stocks, bonds, and corporate class mutual funds.

Capital losses can be used to offset realized capital gains but not any other form of income. They can be used in the current tax year or carried back three years and can be carried forward indefinitely. There is a $750,000 lifetime capital gains exemption for qualified farm property, qualified fishing property or shares in a small business corporation. There is no capital gain on the sale of your principal residence. However, other real estate or property will be subject to capital gain or loss upon disposition.

Tax-exempt income

Some forms of income are not subject to taxation. Gifts or inheritances, life insurance proceeds, personal injury awards and lottery winnings are common examples. Veterans' disability pensions and child tax benefits are government-source payments that are non-taxable.

Some social benefits such as Workers' Compensation, the Guaranteed Income Supplement, and Spouse's Allowance are not taxable but must be considered in net income for the purpose of calculating refundable and non-refundable tax credits.

Keeping Your Net Income Figure Low

One of the components within the Six-Step Plan involves determining the amount of monthly after-tax cash flow that you will need. That number then becomes your income target—the amount that needs to be created from the income sources you have. In terms of personal assets, people will have varying amounts of RRSP, pension, locked-in accounts and non-registered assets. By non-registered I simply mean investments that are not tax sheltered. These would be amounts that are invested from after-tax money. Investment earnings may be exposed to taxation if this money is not invested in tax-efficient vehicles such as TFSAs, corporate class mutual funds or cash-value life insurance.

The key to reaching your target in a tax-efficient manner is to "layer" your income from your benefits and assets using a combination of fully-taxable, tax-favoured and non-taxable sources and to keep your net income figure low. I don't mean as low as possible. You could do that by simply using only non-registered assets and deferring all of the taxable ones. While that may work brilliantly for a few initial years, it could create real tax problems down the road. What I do mean is developing an income strategy that will assist in keeping the net income figure relatively low throughout your retirement.

Remember, your net income is the figure arrived at when you subtract all of your allowable deductions from your total income. It is an important number because it is used in calculating eligibility for income-tested benefits, such as the Canada child tax benefit, goods and services tax/harmonized sales tax credit, social benefits repayment and certain non-refundable tax credits.

Retirement income planners watch the level of net income closely, because in retirement the higher the level of net income:

- the greater the reduction in the age amount and age credit (in excess of $32,961)
- the greater the reduction in OAS payments (in excess of $67,668)
- the higher the deductibles or co-insurance portion for provincial drug programs
- the higher the patient per diem for long-term care facilities

In 2011, for an individual who is aged 65 or over, the absolute "sweet spot" in terms of amount of net income is $32,961. Why do I refer to that benchmark dollar amount as the sweet spot? Once net income exceeds this level, the age amount, which is used to factor the age credit, begins to be reduced (see Age Amount and Credit section above). So by keeping below that level of net income, you are going to have the full benefit of this valuable tax credit. In addition, all of the retirement income for this year will be taxed at the lowest possible marginal rate.

Now, in reality many retirees over the age of 65 find that they do lose some of the age amount simply because their net income is beyond the level where the reduction starts. The key though is to not lose more than is necessary either now or in the future. In looking to avoid needless loss of this entitlement, we need to examine what you might do before age 65 to preserve more of the age amount and OAS after age 65, which may involve taking income from your RRSPs earlier than you had previously thought.

TABLE 8.3 How the Type of Income Affects the 2011 Net Income Calculation

	Type of Income		
	Interest	**Eligible Dividends**	**Realized Capital Gains**
Amount Received	$10,000	$10,000	$10,000
Tax Treatment	fully taxable	grossed-up	50% taxable
Net Income Value	$10,000	$14,100	$5,000

So, clearly, if you are trying to keep the amount of net income relatively low, realized capital gains can play a big role in helping you to achieve that. More to the point, if having these taxable distributions from your non-registered assets added to your other, fully-taxable, sources of retirement income is not attractive or efficient, is there anything you can do? Yes, there are a few different considerations, which I examine in Part Three.

Reducing Your Total Income Through Deductions and Credits

Understanding the difference between a tax deduction and a tax credit will enable you and your advisor to apply strategies and employ financial tools to help you reduce the tax you pay on your retirement income. Tax deductions are subtracted from total income to arrive at the net and taxable income figures. Any deduction serves to lower the net or taxable income figure. This has a positive effect on your income tax calculation since it will reduce tax at the highest marginal rate. As such, the value of a tax deduction increases as your income increases.

Tax credits operate differently. Once calculated, the basic federal tax is reduced by federal tax credits, which include the personal credit, age and pension credits, dividend tax credit, spousal credit and medical expense credit. The resulting number is the federal tax payable. A credit is actually more beneficial than a deduction at lower income levels because it is a dollar-for-dollar reduction in tax payable at the lowest marginal rate. I am going to look more closely at two important tax credits that apply directly to your retirement income planning and your blueprint, the pension credit and the age credit. In retirement, when you are drawing your income from assets and benefits, few tax deductions are available unless you also have employment or rental income. So tax credits become an even more valuable commodity. To lose or waste them needlessly, at any point through the Income Continuum, is extremely inefficient.

Pension Income Amount and Credit

This credit is applied to your first $2,000 of *eligible* income, which is defined as being from the following sources:

At age 65 and over
- periodic receipts from a RRIF, LIF, LRIF, RLIF or PRIF
- formal pension income
- life annuity payments purchased with RRSP proceeds
- periodic annuity payments from DPSP
- interest portion of a non-registered annuity (immediate or deferred)

Under age 65
- formal pension income at any age

You may also have eligible income for this credit if you received the payments because of the death of your spouse or common-law partner and they had been entitled.

Income that does *not* qualify includes CPP, OAS, Guaranteed Income Supplement (GIS) and lump-sum withdrawals from an RRSP. Payments must be on a scheduled, periodic basis. For example, a monthly, quarterly or annual payment from a RRIF would be eligible for the pension credit, but lump-sum withdrawals from an RRSP would not. Non-registered investment income (with the exception of the taxable portion of non-registered annuities) or rental income are also ineligible. The pension credit is applicable to federal tax. When provincial tax credits are also factored in, this is worth approximately $420 to $580 in terms of taxes that you do not have to pay, depending on your province of residence.

This tax credit is not affected by your level of net income (means tested). It is dependent on having a qualifying type of income and on your age. The same sources of income that are eligible for the pension credit also qualify for pension splitting.

Age Amount and Credit

Individuals aged 65 or older by the end of the tax year will qualify for the age credit. It is factored on the age amount and can effectively increase your personal exemption. In 2011, the age amount is $6,537. So if you were entitled to the entire age amount, coupled with your personal exemption of $10,527, your federal "tax-free zone" (income you can earn before you begin paying tax on it) would be $17,064. Increase that number by an additional $2,000 for the pension credit, and you are just over $19,000 before income becomes taxable in 2011. That is if you are entitled to the full age amount. However, once your net income exceeds $32,961, the age amount (and credit) starts to be reduced and is totally eliminated at the point where net income reaches $76,537.

Unused credits are transferable to the spouse. If you do not need all of the age credit to reduce your federal income tax to zero, you can transfer the unused portion of these credits to your spouse.

Other credits, such as the medical expense tax credit and caregiver credit are discussed in detail under Health Risk Management at www.boomersblueprint.com.

MAKING YOUR BLUEPRINT WORK FOR YOU

1. As stated at the outset, for many retirees taxes represent one of the largest personal expenses they have. When I look for areas where improvements can be made, many involve making things more tax efficient. I see lots of articles in financial papers about what people pay in management fees on their investments. But that is a minor issue compared to what is needlessly paid in taxes. Let me repeat:

tax-efficient delivery of the net cash flow you need is a true form of asset preservation.

2. Different forms of income are taxed in different ways and at different rates within the various tax brackets. It is important that you use the least tax-efficient forms of income—CPP, OAS, pension, LIF, RRSP/RRIF—at the lowest tax rates. Tax-favoured and non-taxable sources of income can then be layered on top of these. Yes, use your tax-favoured sources of income (non-registered assets, TFSA, return of capital or corporate class mutual funds, non-registered variable annuities and prescribed annuities—all discussed in detail in Chapter 10) in the higher tax brackets. It is so basic and logical, yet I can't even begin to tell you how often we see this being done improperly.

3. As a retiree, your opportunity for actual deductions from your taxable income are few unless you have employment or rental income. As a result, the tax credits available to you, particularly after age 65, are a very valuable commodity. You should be vigilant to preserve and have the ability to use as many of these as possible. Some may be lost due to your level of taxable or net income, but the point here is that these should not be lost needlessly. And this is an objective that you should have throughout your retirement.

4. A large part of preserving tax credits, as well as other government entitlements such as OAS, has to do with keeping your level of net income low. This is why the efficient layering of your income using taxable and tax-effective sources is important. It is also why you need to be aware of how your assets are being used or deferred, both in the short term and in the future. As was discussed in the previous chapter, deferring all of your registered assets can create real tax problems in the future and could eliminate many credits and entitlements that you would otherwise have been receiving.

9

TAX PLANNING

Putting the Least Amount of Strain on Your Assets

So what is the relationship between the tax treatment on different forms of income and the various tax brackets? The following table examines this by calculating how much pre-tax money would be needed from each type of income in 2011 in order to get $1.00 after tax. I am illustrating a simple combined federal/provincial rate.

TABLE 9.1 Generating One After-Tax Dollar

Tax Bracket	Combined Tax Rate	Fully Taxable*	Eligible Dividends	Capital Gains	TFSA
$10,528–$41,544	20.8%	$1.27	$1.00	$1.12	$1.00
$41,545–$83,088	31.1%	$1.45	$1.09	$1.18	$1.00
$83,089–$128,000	43.4%	$1.76	$1.26	$1.28	$1.00
$128,801 and over	46.4%	$1.86	$1.33	$1.29	$1.00

* Includes CPP, OAS, pensions, income from all registered plans, such as RRIFs, LIFs and interest earned on non-registered investments.

Rule number one of layering your income is: use the least tax-efficient sources of income first. Some people think that they should use up all of their non-registered money first since it is tax exposed and defer all of their RRSP money to use later since it is tax sheltered. While deferral is an effective strategy, you need to assess which assets are best to defer and, in most cases, it is your non-registered holdings, not your RRSPs.

Refer back to Table 8.3 to understand why fully-taxable dollars should be used to establish your base income up to at least the start of the second tax bracket ($41,545 in 2011). In that lowest bracket, you would only need to withdraw $1.27 from a fully-taxable source in order to have $1.00 after tax. Once you are in the next tax bracket (over $41,544), a withdrawal of $1.45 would be needed from a source that was fully taxable to get that same $1.00 after tax. That rise from $1.27 to $1.45 represents a 66.7 per cent increase in tax payable, just to get the next after-tax dollar to spend.

It is then preferable to use tax-favoured or non-taxable forms of income once you are over the first federal bracket, assuming, of course, that you have non-registered assets. You can see how much less dividend income or realized capital gain is required to end up with $1.00 to spend. This will put less strain on your income-producing assets and help to conserve and preserve them. From an efficiency perspective, it is usually preferable to have non-registered investment returns in the form of capital gains rather than dividends. When you look at the previous table, dividends may appear to be the preferable type of income. But remember that the dividend tax credit gross-up inflates your net income figure. What you ultimately want to do is create the amount of after-tax cash flow that you require while keeping your net income figure relatively low.

For more affluent Canadians, it may be appropriate to be referring to taking income to the start of the third tax bracket instead of the second. The numbers may be different but the principles and the strategies are the same. A truly effective blueprint will show a combination of fully-taxable income at the lower tax rates with tax-efficient income at higher tax rates to create the after-tax cash flow you need.

Paying the Piper

One of the changes that occurs when you start drawing your retirement income is how tax is paid on the income. During your working years, tax is deducted by your employer and remitted on your behalf. You are left with your net take-home pay. In retirement, however, that is a factor that you must look after yourself or in conjunction with your advisor or institution. And you will have several sources of income where this needs to be done. Direct remittance of tax is available on any form of income, including government retirement benefits.

It is important to approximate the total tax payable and deduct appropriate amounts from the various payments being made, especially in the first year of retirement. Failure to do this will result in a tax bill in the spring. If you have a non-registered investment account, money could be taken from it to pay the taxes due. But some people face a situation where they have to pull money from RRSP accounts. Although this solves the problem of the current tax bill, it creates larger tax issues for the following year. Direct remittance is particularly important in situations where retirement income begins mid-year, after several months of employment income has been received. It is likely that larger amounts will need to be remitted for the balance of that year.

Institutions holding and making payments to you from your registered income vehicles, such as your RRIF, LIF, LRIF, RLIF or PRIF, are required to withhold and remit taxes based on the level of payments made to you over the course of the year. The withholding schedule is as follows.

TABLE 9.2: Registered Income Withholding Schedule

Amount Withdrawn	Amount Withheld	Quebec Only *
$0–$5,000	10%	5%
$5,001–$15,000	20%	10%
$15,001 and higher	30%	15%

*Plus provincial tax

For periodic income payments, no tax is withheld until the minimum withdrawal amount is exceeded. So, if only the minimum withdrawal is made, then there would be no automatic withholding. Since the minimum withdrawal amount increases each year, the older the recipient, the greater the amount of income from these sources that is not subject to withholding tax. This can be addressed by requesting, via Government of Canada tax form TD3, that a flat percentage be remitted on the entire payment. The form can be completed and submitted at the time the income stream begins or even after payments have started. The amount of deduction can be adjusted by simply filing a new form.

It is not the responsibility of the institution or the government agency making the payments to deduct the correct amount of tax for you. Obviously the sources of these payments do not know all of the other income you are receiving and what is being remitted from those different sources. The amounts to be deducted and remitted should be determined with input from you, your advisor and, if applicable, your accountant. The same withholding formula applies to lump-sum withdrawals from RRSPs; however, the minimum withdrawal exemption does not apply.

The Four *D*s of Effective Tax Planning

Every tax guide or manual makes reference to what are commonly known as "the three *D*s" of effective tax planning: deduct, divide and defer. I am going to add a fourth item. These same principles apply to both the accumulation of assets in pre-retirement years and the income strategies in the retirement years.

Deduct

Anything that you have the opportunity to deduct lowers the amount of your total income and assists you in arriving at a lower taxable income. A $100 deduction means a tax saving of $21 to $46, depending on your taxable income and province of residence. There are a number of allowable deductions, including such major items as registered pension plan contributions, RRSP contributions, and carrying charges and interest expenses on qualifying loans.

Divide

Financial strategies that contribute to this type of effective tax planning include the use of spousal RRSPs and jointly held property. If both partners in a marriage have employment income, there is the opportunity to place non-registered accumulations in the name of the person with fewer assets. Normally assets are divided as they are being accumulated. This is simply a function of placing them in the name of one person or the other. If you have a spouse or partner, you may also have jointly held investments. There are also a number of opportunities to enhance the splitting of income, assets and entitlements at retirement. The major opportunity comes in the form of pension splitting. Details on this appear later in the chapter.

Defer

Deferring the realization, and ultimately the payment, of tax is a benefit to you because it keeps your money working for you longer, rather than reducing it as you go along. By doing so, your investments may have doubled or tripled by the time a disposition occurs and tax must be paid. There may also be a benefit when the tax payable is realized. If the deferral period takes you into your retirement years or years where you experience a lower taxable income, you may also be in a lower income tax bracket when the tax is payable.

Among the tools that allow you to defer taxation are registered pension plan contributions, RRSP contributions and DPSP contributions. For non-registered assets, you can defer taxes by using TFSAs, cash value life insurance, corporate class mutual funds or any capital property that allows you to defer realizing a capital gain. Although the concept of deferral is an important one, you need to be careful which assets you defer. As discussed, there are rules and restrictions on how you can defer registered money. Remember that in addition to these restrictions, any income coming from registered sources is fully taxable. There is ample opportunity to effectively tax defer the growth on non-registered investments, and this area is one that more people need to investigate and develop. Strategies for this appear in Part Three.

Discount

Discounting refers to the use of insurance vehicles to pay for future contingencies and liabilities rather than using your own income and assets for such costs. For example, you can provide tax-free dollars to cover potential costs of future health-related care and taxes. These benefits can be delivered for pennies on the dollar through insurance vehicles. Whether you are using life insurance, critical illness insurance or long-term health-care coverage, the dramatically lower cost and the tax-efficiency of these tools create the fourth *D* in tax planning.

The key point here is that retirement is not the time where you want to be uninsured for health-related costs. Why would you use your own cash flow and assets for these costs when there are insurance vehicles that can do this on a cost-effective and tax-effective basis?

These four Ds are critical elements in creating an effective tax plan, and thereby limiting the negative effects that taxation has on your income. Deduct, divide, defer and discount come up throughout this book.

Pension Splitting

As listed above, "Divide" is one of the four Ds of effective tax planning that can be employed to allow a household to keep more of its pre-tax income. Stated another way, effective tax planning through income splitting allows you to create the after-tax income you require while using less of your own resources. The purpose behind creating two income streams rather than one is really quite simple—there are tax savings to be realized if you have two taxpayers instead of one and particularly where one person's income is significantly greater than the other's. Each person has their own set of exemptions, deductions and credits. In addition, when you can move a taxpayer from a higher tax bracket to a lower tax bracket, savings obviously follow.

The 2007 federal budget introduced a measure known as "pension splitting." This move represented a large shift from previous federal tax policy and created the potential for meaningful tax savings for spouses and common-law partners who are in receipt of eligible pension income, whether they are retired or not. There is no age limit for this to apply, nor does employment status have any effect. A "pensioner" is anyone who is in receipt of eligible pension income and resident in Canada on December 31. The sources of eligible pension income are listed previously in this section under the heading Pension Income Amount and Credit.

Here is a simple explanation of how it works: basically, at the time you jointly file your income tax returns, you can split up to 50% of the eligible pension income from one tax payer to another. It is really not much more complicated than that. It is a year-by-year election and there may be times where it makes sense to split more or less income, but in any case, you cannot exceed 50%.

So what is the benefit of this to you? Pension splitting may help you to keep your "net income" figure low, which in turn will help you preserve more government benefits and entitlements than would otherwise be the case. You may be able to move some income into a lower tax bracket and consequently pay less tax. Let's look at some specific scenarios in order to quantify the tax benefits of pension splitting. I will assume that all people in these examples are over the age of 65 and I will use a sample federal/provincial tax rate.

Scenario One: A single tax payer with a taxable income of $60,000 would pay $12,169 of tax.

Scenario Two: Let's assume we have a couple and each of them has $30,000 of taxable income. Each would pay $2,757 of tax or $5,514 in total. So for the same total household income of $60,000, when the income is split, the total tax owing is less than half of that paid by an individual. That is the benefit of pension splitting. That is a huge difference. This is because a couple over age 65 would each have entitlement to the personal amount ($10,527), the full age amount ($6,537) and the pension credit ($2,000). Add those up, and you have a situation where they each have $19,064 of tax-free income. The remaining amount between $19,065 and $30,000 would be taxed at the lowest combined federal/provincial rate. Now that is efficiency. (All figures based on 2011 numbers.)

But as attractive as this comparison is, it also points out the fact that the tax system discriminates against single retirees.

The last calculation that shows the benefits of pension splitting is to illustrate how this works when you are simply shifting some income from a higher income spouse to a lower income spouse. This is exactly the type of situation that pension splitting was designed to improve. Imagine one person has $60,000 of taxable income and the other has $30,000, for a total household income of $90,000. Also assume that the individual earning $60,000 has eligible income for pension splitting equal to $30,000. Without pension splitting, total taxes payable would be $12,169 + $2,757 = $14,926. Pension splitting would result in them paying only $13,790 ($6,895 x 2), and realizing an annual tax saving of $1,136.

Income Splitting with Non-Registered Assets

There is only one source of non-registered income that is eligible for the pension credit and for pension splitting (after age 65), and that is the interest portion of an immediate or deferred annuity. A GIC issued by a life insurance company is technically a deferred annuity. I do not advocate the use of GICs for your non-registered assets. But, you may wish to use them as part of your investment mix in your non-registered accounts. Well, if you acquire them through a life insurance company and you are age 65 or over, the interest earned is eligible for both the pension credit and for pension splitting. That is not the case with any other issuer such as a bank, trust or mortgage company or credit union.

There are no other opportunities to pension split the income from non-registered assets. How else can you shift income from non-registered investments? While there are a couple of different strategies that involve annually moving smaller amounts of money from one spouse to another over time, it is not my intent to discuss those as the impact is not immediate or meaningful. The one strategy that allows an unlimited amount of non-registered capital to be moved from one spouse to another is the Spousal Loan. There are no dollar amount limits or age restrictions, but there is a process that must be followed and documentation that must be in place.

For our example, I will use a married retired couple, Marvin and Tammy, where she is the higher income recipient. She also has $300,000 of non-registered assets in her name and is looking for some method of having less taxable income in her name.

To create a spousal loan, proper documentation must be in place. A signed acknowledgement of the loan should be maintained in your files and should include the following information:

- date of loan
- amount of proceeds to be loaned
- interest rate to be applied to outstanding balance
- repayment terms to allow interest-only payments
- date by which interest payments are due
- structure (a demand loan with no defined term)
- provision that the loan can be terminated and full repayment made with notice from either the borrower or the lender
- signatures of all parties involved

The CRA permits this type of loan as long as certain interest rate and payment conditions are met:

- The lender must charge interest to the borrower. The interest rate can be set by the lender but cannot be less than the prescribed rate established quarterly by the CRA. At the time of writing, the minimum or prescribed rate is at an historical low of 1 per cent. It is important to note that once the loan is in place, the rate of interest applies as long as the loan is in place, regardless of future changes to the prescribed rate.
- Payment of loan interest must be made and documented. The best way to accomplish documentation is to have loan interest paid by cheque. Interest is calculated to the end of the calendar year and must be paid by January 31 of the next year. Once the loan is established, it can stay in place indefinitely or it can be easily wound up with repayment to the lender.

So, back to our example:

- Tammy loans Marvin $300,000.
- He immediately invests this money (any investment returns from this point forward are taxed in Marvin's hands, not Tammy's).
- Marvin will pay Tammy $3,000 at the end of the year (assuming a full year's interest).

- The $3,000 is taxable to Tammy as income.
- Since Marvin used the loan to purchase taxable investments, the interest he pays to Tammy should a tax deductible expense for him.
- Since Marvin has the lower taxable income, any taxable distributions from his investments will be taxed at his lower rate.

Whether this strategy makes financial sense to initiate, and if so, to what extent, will be determined by the specifics in each situation.

MAKING YOUR BLUEPRINT WORK FOR YOU

Okay, here is one very profound comment before I summarize this section: remember that it is always better to have a tax problem than an income problem. With that bit of wisdom now firmly embedded in your mind, let me quickly add that there are many things that need to be considered so that your retirement income is created in a tax-efficient manner.

1. We have to pay our share of taxes on income, and that is only fair. What I am trying to put forward here are the things that I encounter as an advisor where people are needlessly paying more tax than they should be. Aside from the resulting obvious waste of your money, it also puts unnecessary stress on your income-producing assets and that, in turn, is a threat to sustaining your retirement income. You need to be sure that your sources of income are set up for you in the most efficient way. How do you do that? Have your advisor explain to you—in detail—how and why they are set up the way that they are. If they can't provide you with that explanation, guess what? There are likely improvements you can find by working through another advisor who is proficient in the area of retirement income planning. And you may be very surprised to find out just how significant those improvements can be for you.

2. Most people understand defer, deduct and divide when it comes to three of the four *D*s of tax efficiency. Where they miss the mark is on the fourth *D*, which is discount. This refers to the use of insurance to cover health-related costs. This could be something as simple as dental and prescription drug costs or more significant issues involving long-term care or critical illness. Investigate how insurance may very effectively cover these potential liabilities and allow you more discretion with how you use your money in retirement.

3. Deferral of taxation is a very effective tax strategy, and the questions that need to be answered are:

   - Which assets are best to defer?
   - Which assets are the best to use?
   - What is the best combination of income sources to make this work efficiently over the duration of the Income Continuum?
   - Are there additional amounts of taxable income that should be converted to non-registered assets?

4. Your goal is to make most efficient use of your income-producing assets. This means creating the after-tax cash flow you need while keeping the taxable income, or net income, figure low. The ability to split income may go a long way toward this goal if there is a disparity in the amounts of income between two spouses or partners.

5. For those age 65 and over, the only form of eligible pension income for non-registered assets is the interest portion of an immediate or deferred annuity. In the case of income annuities, this applies whether you are using a life annuity or a term-certain annuity. Should you find that you have too many non-registered assets in one person's name, there are strategies that can shift ownership to your spouse.

PART

FIVE

SPECIAL TOOLS AND STRATEGIES

10

WITH A LITTLE HELP FROM MY FRIENDS

The Four Investment Considerations

I started my career in the life insurance business in 1978, fresh out of university. In those days, part of new-agent training was making a presentation that allowed you to describe what you did and what you could offer to prospective new clients. When I look back at it today, the messages in that presentation were simple and yet so very true. One of the sections of that presentation addressed the three financial dangers: being unable to work due to a disability, dying too soon or living too long. In those days, at age 24, I really didn't think that much about the latter of those three hazards. Now, of course, it is front and centre in the work that I do creating blueprints for clients and delivering the income they need.

How do I combine strategies and financial tools that deliver the comfort people need—knowing they won't outlive their income and at the same time providing the flexibility that is so important at this time in their lives? There are a lot of factors that go into developing and implementing the solutions. From a financial perspective, both you and your advisor need to discuss and evaluate the weightings, or emphasis, you wish to put on each of the following four key investment considerations.

1. Certainty

I am referring to providing a guaranteed income that you know will not decrease or cease. You may want to be certain that your income can cover a specific time period or that you won't outlive it. This type of income stream, once started, will not be affected by changes in interest rates or the stock market.

2. Probability

This implies that you are using a variable investment portfolio, which will fluctuate in value, either up or down, based on investment returns. That change in value may also result in an increase or decrease in the level of income that you either can or wish to receive. You and your advisor must determine the probability that both the life of the asset plus the income generated from it will be sustainable, as long as the rate of return and the withdrawal rate are realistically and proportionately aligned (discussed as Sustainability in Chapter 4).

3. Flexibility

Does the financial tool allow you to make changes? Is it flexible? Can income be increased or decreased? Can you access sums of capital if that became necessary? If you change your mind or if your situation changes after you acquire it, can you alter or discontinue it?

4. Perpetuity

What are the financial implications for the survivor, the beneficiaries and the estate with any of the tools chosen?

All financial tools will have different degrees of strength and weakness in these four areas. Defining your priorities in these four areas will play a large role in determining which solutions will work best and how they may work together in helping you to fulfill your objectives.

FIGURE 10.1: Four Considerations

CERTAINTY

PROBABILITY   **PERPETUITY**

FLEXIBILITY

I have shown these four considerations in the above manner to illustrate that they do not flow in the same direction. At times, there may be complementary factors between them. For example, a variable investment portfolio that functions on probability may also have a great deal of flexibility. But more commonly, they are pulling in opposite directions. A financial tool that delivers certainty may not provide flexibility. Ultimately, the selection of the tools that are used as solutions will largely be driven by your biases and preferences, as well as the biases and preferences of your advisor, relating to these four considerations.

The Three Headwinds

There are other factors that also have an impact on the ultimate effectiveness, fit and performance of a financial tool as a solution. I refer to these factors as "headwinds." As the name suggests, these are factors that have the potential to inhibit or "to be a drag" on the effectiveness of any one solution. That is why it sometimes makes great sense to look at combining financial tools and strategies to cover off a number of the four considerations and deal with the headwinds. The most significant headwinds that impede the effectiveness of various financial tools are taxation, inflation and fees.

Taxation

How tax-efficient is the solution? This has to do with a number of measures: How is the cash flow treated in terms of taxation? How much of the payment is taxable and how is it taxed? How effectively does the vehicle defer taxation? Does it assist or hinder your efforts to preserve government benefits and entitlements as much as possible?

Inflation

Does the solution provide a mechanism or the potential to address future inflation issues?

Fees

Comparatively, how do the fee structures measure up? The industry runs on fees. Our services and our offices run on fees. People have to be paid for their services one way or another, and the financial industry is no different. That said, what are the fees? Are they reasonable? Is any portion of the fee deductible? What are the fees that you pay intended to provide to you? Are you getting what you are paying for?

The four considerations and three headwinds can be used to evaluate any investment portfolio and/or income tool. This could include an ETF portfolio, mutual funds or pools, segregated funds or individual stocks and bonds. But there are some additional tools and strategies that have specific application to income planning. So in this part of the book I look at some of the tools that help to deliver efficient solutions and the strategies involved in their use. I compare how they measure up in terms of the four considerations and how they are impacted by and may be expected to address the three headwinds. There are things here that you may have heard of before, but I want to help you understand them and how they may work effectively for you.

Corporate Class (Capital Class) Funds

Normally, when you place money in a mutual fund, your investment dollars purchase units of the fund. This is because the legal status of a mutual fund is a unit trust. But corporate class funds are a series of different mutual funds, each representing a class of shares of a larger corporation. Each corporate class is a separate investment fund, but all classes fall under the umbrella of the holding corporation. This structure was really designed for non-registered investments and has been in existence since 1987. Today, almost all fund companies have a corporate class version of their offerings, and if you have non-registered investments, there are many reasons why you would be better served to have them in this structure.

First, one of the significant differences between this legal status and that of unit trusts is that the exchange of different classes of shares within the same corporation is not viewed as a disposition for tax purposes. In essence, a corporate class fund, or pool, allows investors the flexibility to make the same type of trading and investment decisions as they would make with their RRSP, yet with no immediate taxes triggered from a trade.

In this regard, the "corporation" provides the same benefits for open money as the RRSP shelter provides for registered funds. This provides very tax-efficient flexibility. Assume that you have made a meaningful gain on some "Canadian Class" shares and wish to move some or all of these holdings to the "American Class." Unlike a regular unit trust mutual fund, there is no taxable disposition to make that trade. Even if you move the entire account to the "Money Market Class" of shares, no capital gain will be realized until you have income or lump sums paid out to you.

Second, the corporate structure allows the fund company to manage potential earnings and losses to reduce taxable income from distributions generated by the classes of the corporation. This has historically resulted in very few, if any, taxable distributions to the investor.

Third, some fund companies have money market, fixed income and balanced fund options under their corporate class structure. Any gain that is realized when money is drawn out from these investments will be received from the corporate class fund or pool almost exclusively as a taxable capital gain. And this tends to be the most efficient form of taxation. Capital gains also has the least impact on raising the amount of net income on your tax return. And that is very positive. So the corporate class structure not only serves as an effective shelter for interest income, but also "converts" it to a capital gain when taxation does occur. These are not perfect shelters and are not promoted as such. But they are an exceptionally efficient tool when investing non-registered money.

To a large extent, the corporate class structure acts as a mechanism to defer taxation and provides you with a far greater amount of control over when and how the money from your non-registered assets is taxed. After funding TFSAs, I use the corporate class structure for investing the additional after-tax amounts that are purposefully taken from RRSP/RRIF accounts in the quest to intelligently disassemble things for people.

An additional advantage of this structure involves streaming income from a corporate class account. Through what is commonly known as a "T-series option," monthly payments of non-taxable return of capital can be made to maximize tax efficiency and provide a stream of consistent cash flow. Withdrawal amounts usually range from 4 to 8 per cent annually and can be easily tailored to your needs.

Just like any other mutual fund, the corporate class investments can be set up on what is called an "F-series fee structure." This is an unbundling of the components of the management expense ratio (MER). The overall management expense ratio stays about the same if the advisor adds full retail compensation. But in the unbundled approach that the F-series provides, the portion of the overall fee that is paid to the advisor is generally accepted as a deductible expense for tax purposes. (That is on non-registered investments only.) So imagine, this structure limits taxable distributions and provides a deductible investment expense at the same time. That is a very favourable combination of features.

The corporate class structure, with all of the features it offers, is a tremendous tool to use, either on its own or in tandem with other financial tools.

Life Annuities: How Mortality Credits Can Help You

I used to say, "In the retirement income market, capital preservation is king." And while there is still merit to that comment, the reality is that sustainability of income is actually more important than capital preservation.

Life annuities are discussed in detail in Chapter 6 as one of the income options for pensions. Here I'm focusing on a life annuity that is purchased later in life rather than at the more common retirement age. This is so that I can show you the positive impact of mortality credits, which come into play when life annuities are purchased at older ages. Just about everyone knows that as you get older, the premiums for life insurance get higher. While aging is not good when it comes to buying life insurance, the opposite is true when buying your life annuity, thanks to mortality credits. They meaningfully increase the amount of income that you can receive from an annuity (see tables 10.2, 10.3 and 10.4)

In fact, when you are in your late seventies, mortality credits become a more important factor when calculating annuity income than do prevailing interest rates. The mortality credit increases with age, thereby creating a higher amount of income for the same amount of capital. This also serves to hedge longevity risk. The resulting level of guaranteed income that can be created would be impossible to match in the broader financial markets.

How significant is this in a time of extremely low interest rates? In 2009, the leading issuer of life annuities in the United States sold over one billion dollars' worth of new life annuity business. More than 50 per cent of those annuities were sold to individuals aged 80 and over!

Table 10.2 shows monthly income from a $100,000 single life annuity for a male, purchased at various ages with payments guaranteed to age 90. You can see the increasingly positive enhancements in the amount of monthly income to be paid from age 76 onward.

TABLE 10.2: Monthly Income from a Single Life Annuity

Age	Income	Yield	Age	Income	Yield
65	$569	6.83%	76	$605	8.34%
66	$579	6.95%	77	$726	8.71%
67	$589	7.07%	78	$761	9.13%
68	$600	7.20%	79	$801	9.61%
69	$610	7.32%	80	$846	10.15%
70	$621	7.45%	81	$899	10.79%
71	$631	7.57%	82	$960	11.52%
72	$641	7.69%	83	$1,029	12.35%
73	$650	7.80%	84	$1,109	13.31%
74	$659	7.91%	85	$1,208	14.50%
75	$667	8.01%	Guaranteed to 90		

Incomes and yields shown for a life annuity guaranteed 15 years from purchase. Starting at age 76, guarantee period is shown to age 90.

Table 10.3 repeats the income and yield figures from the above table for age 76 and beyond where a guarantee period is involved. Then it compares the same income and yield calculations for the purchase of a life annuity with no guarantee period.

TABLE 10.3: Monthly Income from a Single Life Annuity (Guaranteed)

Age	Income	Yield	Age	Income	Yield
76	$695	8.34%	76	$903	10.84%
77	$726	8.71%	77	$942	11.30%
78	$761	9.13%	78	$984	11.81%
79	$801	9.61%	79	$1,029	12.35%
80	$846	10.15%	80	$1,079	12.95%
81	$899	10.79%	81	$1,132	13.58%
82	$960	11.52%	82	$1,189	14.27%
83	$1,029	12.35%	83	$1,250	15.005
84	$1,109	13.31%	84	$1,302	15.62%
85	$1,208	14.50%	85	$1,390	16.68%
Guaranteed to 90			0 Guarantee		

At the same age, both the income and the yield are much higher when no guarantee period is attached. With no guarantee period, there are no more payments nor is there any estate value at the passing of the annuitant.

Table 10.4 makes the same comparison as the previous table, between a life annuity with a guarantee to age 90 and one with no guarantee, but is based on a joint life annuity with a female spouse who is two years younger than her husband.

TABLE 10.4: Monthly Income from a Joint Life Annuity

Male	Income	Yield	Male	Income	Yield
76	$620	7.44%	76	$657	7.88%
77	$641	7.69%	77	$679	8.15%
78	$655	7.86%	78	$703	8.44%
79	$680	8.16%	79	$729	8.75%
80	$707	8.48%	80	$757	9.08%
81	$750	9.00%	81	$788	9.46%
82	$772	9.26%	82	$821	9.85%
83	$810	9.72%	83	$857	10.28%
84	$852	10.22%	84	$895	10.74%
85	$912	10.94%	85	$936	11.23%
Guaranteed to 90			0 Guarantee		

Tables 10.2, 10.3 and 10.4 reflect rates in effect January 2010

So, let's revisit Jack and Diane and his pension decision from Chapter 6. Assume that he had chosen a Life Income Fund and had experienced a 5 per cent return over the time he had his money invested. At age 80, the balance in his LIF account is $264,000. The income from the LIF starts to decline at this point. If that trend of declining income started to become a concern, he could purchase a life annuity with some, or all, of the money in his LIF account. With that capital balance, Jack could acquire a joint life annuity with no income reduction for Diane following Jack's death that paid $1,920 monthly for as long as either of them is alive. Had he purchased the same form of annuity at age 62, when he retired, the income would have been $2,270 but would have cost him $500,000, nearly twice the amount. That is the power of mortality credits.

But remember, a life annuity is a principal encroachment vehicle, so capital is going to be used to deliver this level of income over the life of the annuitant. Essentially you will be using up the principal you put into the annuity in exchange for a higher, guaranteed income. A guarantee period can be added to protect the estate but cannot extend past age 90. So if someone purchased a life annuity at age 84, for example, the guarantee period would not extend past age 90. If certainty of sustainable income is a much more important factor than the perpetuity of assets to the estate, then this could be a very valid consideration for some of your retirement capital.

Prescribed Taxation and Prescribed Annuities

A life annuity purchased with non-registered assets can receive preferential tax treatment through what is known as prescribed taxation. In order to qualify for prescribed tax treatment, the annuity must meet the following conditions.

- The original capital must be after-tax money. This could be capital from the proceeds of a life insurance contract, proceeds from the sale of a principal residence or the value of any non-registered investments or capital.
- The annuity can be in any form—term-certain, single life or joint life.

- The contract must be owned by an individual, not a corporation.
- The income cannot be indexed.
- The guarantee period of a life annuity or the end of a term-certain annuity cannot exceed the primary annuitant's age 90.

An annuity is a guaranteed stream of future income payments made up of a combination of principal and interest. In a regular annuity, where conventional taxation applies, the interest payments and hence the taxation are much larger at the beginning and much smaller toward the end. This works like a mortgage in reverse. Think about it. How much principal do you actually reduce in the first five years of a mortgage? Very little. Most of what you're paying is interest.

FIGURE 10.5: Conventional Taxation

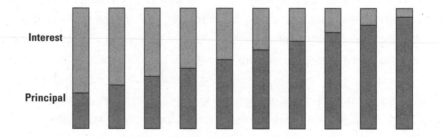

For non-registered capital, prescribed annuities receive very different tax treatment than do regular annuities, and this can work favourably for you. Prescribed tax treatment takes the estimated total interest payments (in the case of a life annuity) or the exact amount of total interest that will be paid (a term-certain annuity) and deems that for each year of the annuity the interest portion will be the same amount. In other words, it levels the interest amount and the tax-free return-of-capital amount for each year of payment. The end result is that there is more tax-effective income in the earlier years.

The total amount of interest to be paid over the duration of the annuity is calculated, then divided over the number of payments in the life of the contract. This would be a straightforward exercise in the case of a term-certain annuity, where the duration of the payments is known, but what about a life annuity? In this case, insurers use the same mortality tables found in the CRA's Interpretation Bulletin IT-111R2 to project a life expectancy. This number of years is deemed to be the life of the contract.

FIGURE 10.6: Prescribed Taxation

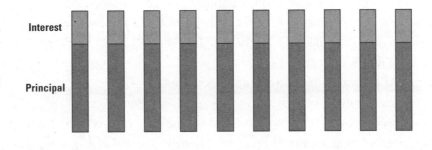

So let's combine an example of prescribed taxation working in harmony with mortality credits. Imagine we acquire a single life annuity (rates as of January 2011) for a female age 75 using $100,000 of non-registered capital. This would purchase a guaranteed lifetime monthly income of $702.35. The income for each year would be $8,428. The taxable amount each year is $465.22. At a 31 per cent tax rate, there would be $144.22 of taxes paid, providing her with a net income of $8,284 yearly from her $100,000 investment. Granted, a large portion of this is the return of her after-tax capital. But if the objective is to have sustainable guaranteed income for life, the alternative of only getting 3.5 per cent interest on a GIC is dramatically different. The $3,500 earned on a GIC is fully taxable and at the same 31 per cent tax rate it would deliver an annual after-tax income of $2,415. That is less than one-third of the net income that the annuity would deliver.

If the desire is to have guaranteed lifetime income and also to provide an estate, then the insured annuity is a concept that may have appeal. That is discussed in the Insured Annuities section.

The Tax-Deferred Annuity

This is not a stand-alone product, but a proven strategy that is designed to address three key objectives for retirement income. It is difficult to generate meaningful guaranteed income in the current low-interest-rate environment. That is further complicated if non-registered assets are creating fully-taxable interest income. And although there is a need for some growth in assets during retirement to address inflation, there is also a bit of lingering trepidation regarding the stock markets after the disaster of 2008 and early 2009. This concept involves combining two of the special tools we have just looked at, the prescribed annuity and corporate class funds. By using these two vehicles in tandem, you can realize the following:

- guaranteed income
- the potential for tax-deferred growth
- a tax efficient-strategy for the above objectives

The example I'm going to use involves a female, age 70, who has just had a non-registered GIC or bond mature for $100,000. She wants guaranteed income but also realizes that there is a need for some growth in her assets. She does not want to purchase a life annuity because she wants to preserve her capital. An insured annuity is not a consideration since she is not able to acquire life insurance. Ideally she would also like to see less tax on her income. She has a 31 per cent marginal tax rate and the GIC renewal rate is 3.5 per cent. Here is how the strategy compares in her situation:

TABLE 10.7: The Tax-Deferred Annuity

GIC @3. 5%		Term-Certain Annuity	Corporate Class Fund
Portfolio			
$100,000	Amount of Capital	$21,281	$78,719
$3,500	Annual Income	$2,540	0
0	Tax-Free Amount	$2,136	0
$3,500	Taxable Amount	$404	0
$1,085	Tax Payable	$125	0
$2,415	Total Net Income	$2,415	0
$100,000	Value at End of Annuity	0	$140,940
	Fund Break-Even Rate	**2.83%**	$100,000
$2,415	Net Income After Annuity Ends		**$7,145**

If she buys a GIC at 3.5 per cent, an income of $3,500 per year will be paid out and the full amount is taxable to her. At a 31 per cent marginal rate, she will pay $1,085 in tax and end up with a net income of $2,415. For the sake of the illustration, I will assume that she is using a five-year GIC, which will have the same rate at renewal both 5 and 10 years from now.

The tax-deferred annuity combines the use of a 10-year certain pre-scribed annuity contract with the purchase of corporate class funds. It takes $21,821 placed in the annuity to equal the annual after-tax income of $2,415 that is created by having $100,000 in a 3.5 per cent GIC or bond (assuming a 31 per cent marginal tax rate.) This creates the same level of guaranteed income, after tax, for 10 years.

The remaining $78,719 is placed into a corporate class fund portfo-lio that can provide some potential for growth and is tax efficient. The assumption in the illustration is that the return on these deferred invest-ments, net of fees and any taxable distributions that may "leak" out, will be 6.0 per cent annualized. This money will have 10 years to grow while the annuity delivers the same guaranteed after-tax income that the GIC or bond would provide. And she would always have access to the investments if she needed to withdraw a lump sum or additional income. She would not likely have this same flexibility with a GIC.

At the end of 10 years, the term-certain annuity would have come to an end. At that same time, the GIC would renew at $100,000 of principal and, assuming that interest rates stayed constant, continue to generate the same $2,415 of after-tax income. The investments, at 6.0 per cent, will have grown to $140,940. I have assumed that there is minimal tax leakage along the way and have adjusted the returns accordingly to net the 6.0 per cent. If she took 6.0 per cent per year from the $140,940, she would receive $8,456. Assuming that this was fully taxable as a capital gain, the after-tax income at a 31 per cent marginal rate would be $7,145. (This does not take into account the adjusted cost base of $78,719, so this income would actually be even more tax-effective than shown here.)

While I have assumed a growth rate of 6 per cent, the investments would have to achieve a return of just 2.83 per cent compounded in order to have a value of $100,000 after taxes at the end of 10 years (which would leave her with the same amount of capital as the maturing GIC). It is also important to note that the amount to be included in her taxable income is $3,500 with the GIC compared to only $404 from the prescribed annuity (plus some potential tax leakage from the investments). The tax-deferred annuity is far more effective in creating the income needed while keeping the net income figure low. This could help to preserve some of her government benefits and entitlements.

This strategy affords her the guarantees she is looking for in a tax-efficient manner. She also has flexibility in that she could access the investment portfolio if she wanted to. In fact, if she wanted a higher guaranteed income at the outset, she could just direct more to the annuity and less to the portfolio. The income stream is guaranteed for the next 10 years and the investment portfolio has 10 full years to stay invested. That longer horizon should take the attention off of the day-to-day movement of the markets.

So, what if the investment portfolio had absolutely no growth over 10 years? The annuity is finished and she needs income. She would have an investment account with a value of $78,719. If the concern is running out of income, what are the options? She set up the tax-deferred annuity when she was 70. Ten years later, at age 80, $78,719 could purchase a life annuity, guaranteed for 10 years, that would pay her $6,961 per year, after tax. Or, using the same type of life annuity, a net annual income of $3,623 could be purchased for $41,265. That would still leave just over $37,454 in her investment account.

Note: This tax-deferred annuity is even more attractive and effective if interest rates are higher and/or when higher marginal tax rates are involved.

Insured Annuities

There are times where the objectives of guaranteed sustainable income and preserving capital for the survivor or the estate have an equal priority. There is a strategy involving non-registered capital that allows you to address both of these objectives in a very efficient way. Once again, it involves combining two financial tools to best obtain the desired outcome. This is also known as a "back-to-back annuity."

Let's examine this using the example of a couple, Desmond (age 65) and Molly (age 62). Both are retired and in the 31 per cent marginal tax bracket. They jointly own $200,000 in a non-registered account. They are disgruntled with the current low yield on this money and further annoyed by the fact that they are taxed on the paltry amount of interest it earns. One option they have is to take these savings and place them in a five-year GIC that will pay them 3.5 per cent. They are not concerned with committing the capital for a period of time, as they have built up some other non-registered savings plus they have each contributed the maximum to their respective TFSA accounts. But they are wondering if there are any alternatives to help them do what they wish to do with this money.

They wish to safely invest this money, preserve the capital and receive a better income in a more tax-efficient way. The following is one strategy involving two financial tools that will help them to meet their objectives. Both are non-smokers and in reasonably good health. Below is the comparative illustration and then the description.

TABLE 10.8: Comparison of GIC Versus Annuity Options

Assumptions: Male age 65, female age 62, both non-smokers, $200,000 principal, GIC rate 3.5%, marginal tax rate 31%

	3.5% GIC	Single Life Annuity*	Joint Life Annuity
Annual Income	$7,000	$14,796	$11,242
Taxable Portion	$7,000	$3,160	$3,351
Tax Paid @31%	($2,100)	($979)	($1,038)
Net Income from Taxable Portion	$4,900	$2,181	$2,313
Non-Taxable Portion	n/a	$11,636	$7,891
Total After-Tax Income	$4,900	$13,817	$10,204
Annual Life Insurance Premium	n/a	($6,114)	($2,710)
Total Net Annual Income	**$4,900**	**$7,703**	**$7,494**
After-Tax Increase over Five-Year GIC Income		57.2%	52.9%
Rate of Return Pre-Tax	3.50%	7.39%	5.62%
Rate of Return After Tax @ 31%	2.45%	3.85%	3.75%

*male age 65
Annuity and life insurance illustration at January 2011

If they place the $200,000 in a conventional GIC with an effective payout rate of 3.5 per cent, the annual income would be $7,000, all of which will be taxable. At their tax rate of 31 per cent, this would create tax payable of $2,100, leaving $4,900 as a net income.

I have included a single life annuity scenario, just for comparative purposes. But Desmond and Molly will be looking at a joint life annuity with level income. The concept is very straightforward. A joint life annuity is purchased so that a guaranteed income of $11,242 is payable on an annual basis for as long as either Desmond or Molly are alive. In order to create the highest possible income, I have illustrated an annuity with no guarantee period. What this means is that when the last surviving annuitant (Desmond or Molly) dies, there will be no benefit to the estate and the heirs. This is why they have acquired a joint last-to-die life insurance contract for $200,000 of benefit. Assuming standard health, the annual premium would be $2,710. Once they have both died, a non-taxable benefit of $200,000 will be paid to named beneficiaries or the estate, thereby replacing the original capital. The estate would be in exactly the same position as if the other investment option, a GIC, had been purchased. The major benefits are realized in the after-tax income that Desmond and Molly will receive for as long as either of them is alive.

In the joint life scenario, even after removing the amount required to fund the insurance, they still have a guaranteed net income of $7,494. This is $2,594 more each year, on an after-tax basis, than current interest rates would provide from a bond or a GIC. This represents an increase in their spendable income of almost 53 per cent. Stated another way, they would have to own a GIC or bond paying an interest rate of 5.5 per cent to deliver the same after-tax income as the joint life annuity.

The illustration uses an insurance contract where premiums are payable until the second death, which is also when the benefit would be paid to the estate. In attempting to implement this strategy, they must know that the insurance coverage can be acquired. This is the obvious first step. Since the coverage is based on a second-to-die strategy, underwriting has some degree of flexibility. It makes sense to apply for the coverage with several carriers since underwriting decisions can vary greatly. Having shopped the market in this manner, Desmond and Molly can obtain the coverage on the most favourable terms. Companies that wish to impose a rating on the insurance or that decline to issue the coverage are then among the best candidates for the annuity purchase. This is because they feel that the individual or couple involved has a shorter-than-average life expectancy. As a result, the life annuity income that could be obtained from these insurers is likely to be higher.

Ultimately, Desmond and Molly receive more after-tax income from the insured annuity than they would from the GIC. That is at current rates. If interest rates start to move up, then they may find themselves at an income level that is less than that which could be provided by a GIC with higher yield. Annuities will provide more income when rates go up but only for new purchases. And therein lies one of the dilemmas with annuity purchases at this point in time. You are buying rates for the next 25 or 30 years and they are basically at historical lows. Do you want to lock yourself into that? That is the risk you take in the current environment. In the example, Desmond and Molly thought it was worthwhile, because once they were both dead, their estate would receive a $200,000 non-taxable payment from the insurance, thereby restoring and preserving the original capital. An added benefit is that the insurance proceeds will flow into the estate directly, circumventing the will, and therefore be exempt from probate.

In addition to the current interest rate environment, the other trade-off in this whole arrangement is that the couple will not have access to the principal if it has been used to purchase an annuity. However, this is not a large issue if the prime focus is to satisfy the guaranteed investment and income objectives stated earlier. That is why it is only suggested for a portion of one's assets or for that amount of capital that is required to create a specific income payment

The New (well, newer) Kid in Town: Variable Annuities

Late in 2006, Manulife Financial introduced Canadians to an income delivery vehicle that has been extremely popular in the United States since 2002. It is a variable annuity with a guaranteed minimum withdrawal benefit (GMWB). Initial response by consumers was very strong, with billions of dollars flowing to this financial tool. We are now at a point in Canada where basically all life insurance companies have a product offering of this type. They go by different product names and there are subtle differences among them, but basically they are "variable annuities." It would take a few pages to describe this product in detail. In fact, the information booklet issued by the life companies to describe the offering to potential investors is larger than this book. Here, however, is an overview of this financial tool.

This product is really a portfolio of segregated funds (mutual funds with an insurance wrapper) that provides a stream of guaranteed income for life. The income amount is set at 5 per cent of the original investment if income commences immediately and you are age 65 or over. For those starting income before age 65, the payout decreases to 4.5 per cent and drops to 4 per cent for those younger than 60. For simplicity, let's look at a scenario where the annuitant is 65 at the time the income begins.

The percentage of guaranteed withdrawal can increase from 5 per cent if the original deposit is made in advance of the time that income commences. For example, if you make your original investment today and start drawing income 10 years from now, there is an enhancement to the 5 per cent guaranteed minimum withdrawal benefit of 5 per cent (of the 5 per cent) per year. In plain English, if there were a full 10 years between the initial investment in this vehicle and the time the income commenced, the GMWB would be 7.5 per cent instead of 5 per cent.

These products are designed to eliminate the danger of depleting principal when withdrawals and negative investment returns occur simultaneously, especially early in retirement (see Chapter 4). In addition to this protection, they allow for "resets" every three years if your investments have performed well and your account balance has increased over and above the original deposit.

The guarantee of an income that you cannot outlive and that will not change has some real appeal. That holds true for those who either don't have an income from pension or don't have a level of guaranteed income that will cover their necessary expenses in retirement. Unlike a conventional life annuity, you can collapse the variable annuity should life circumstances change. For example, the desire to make sure that you don't outlive your retirement income may be a compelling reason for using this financial tool. You could experience a sudden and major decline in your health. If that occurred, then it may very well be that the fear of longevity and running out of money is no longer a large issue for you. You would have the option to collapse the variable annuity, take the capital and use it in a different way. Variable annuities do pay out a lower initial income than conventional annuities. At age 65 this can be 25 to 33 per cent less, but keep in mind that the variable annuity provides a better opportunity for there to be a survivor or estate benefit because of the feature of having an account value.

There are two things about variable annuities to keep in mind. First, although these products offer features of annuities and investment portfolios, they are not "the best of both worlds." The income from a variable annuity is not as high as that which would be provided by a traditional annuity. And the investment portfolio is going to have the drag of higher fees. So while there is a combination of features, these do not include the best aspects of traditional annuities and investments. Second, only a portion of anyone's overall wealth should be dedicated to variable annuities. They should work in tandem with other investment tools and strategies as part of your overall income allocation.

On variable annuities purchased with non-registered capital, income payments will initially be taxed as a refund of principal. This means that there will be no taxation on the income until such time as the sum of payments exceeds the adjusted cost base. Remember that the adjusted cost base is the amount of capital that originally went into the plan. This return of principal is very tax-efficient as an income stream and in line with the principles of layering income that I have discussed. The tax treatment works exactly the same as it does for T-series corporate class funds, which were described earlier in this chapter.

You also need to be aware of the cost of these guarantees. The fund portfolios used within these products have management fees and annuity fees that can run from 3.3 per cent to about 3.9 per cent per year. That is pretty hefty and more costly than regular segregated funds, which have high MERs to begin with to cover the guarantees they provide. All of the marketing illustrations show you how your portfolio and income can increase if the investment return is in excess of the 5 per cent withdrawal. Well, in as much as that is true, that investment return must not only exceed the 5 per cent withdrawal but also the (for example) 3.5 per cent management fee. So your portfolio needs an 8.5 per cent return just to keep the capital intact. This also has to fly in the face of the fact that the most aggressive asset allocation available on the variable portfolio is a 70/30 equity to fixed income mix. When you subtract the return on the fixed income portion from the management fee, you are currently getting next to no return. So the 70 per cent of the portfolio invested in equities is providing all of the returns. That means the equity portion needs to grow at a rate of 12.14 per cent in order to give the portfolio an overall return of 8.5 per cent. While that is possible, it is not as easily done year after year, as recent equity investment returns have shown.

That does not mean that variable annuities aren't good. They are a real option if your objectives dovetail with what these vehicles can provide. You have a combination of guarantees and flexibility, and in retirement income planning, that is a desirable pairing of features. My point is simply this: know what you are acquiring and the cost/benefit relationship that is involved. And don't be surprised, frustrated or disappointed if you are not seeing regular increases in your income every three years, as the marketing material may suggest. The other aspect that this product does provide is peace of mind. If you are drawing your retirement income from the pool of assets that you have saved over your lifetime, you are going to feel much more at ease by having some portion of your income guaranteed.

True, there are some risks, notably the potential insolvency of the insurance issuer. Fortunately, all annuity issuers in Canada must belong to Assuris, a not-for-profit organization that protects Canadian policyholders. If the insurance company goes bankrupt, up to $2,000 per month or 85 per cent of the promised income benefit, whichever is higher, is assured.

Comparing the Options

So let's compare what we have just looked at from the perspective of the four considerations identified earlier. They all have different combinations of strengths and weaknesses, which I have rated on a scale of 1 to 5. The higher the number, the greater the strength. For every individual or couple there is going to be a personal weighting and preference for these considerations. Remember that the best overall solution for you may involve a combination of these tools since they have strengths in different areas. Below this table, I will provide comment on how these tools address the three headwinds.

TABLE 10.9: Comparison of the Special Tools Using the Four Investment Considerations

	Corporate Class Funds	Prescribed Annuity	Tax-Deferred Annuity	Insured Annuity	Variable Annuity
Certainty	3	5	4	5	5
Probability	3	5	4.5	5	5
Flexibility	5	1	4	1	4
Perpetuity	3.5	1	4	5	3.5

Inflation

TABLE 10.10 Comparison of the Special Tools Using One of the Three Headwinds

	Corporate Class Funds	Prescribed Annuity	Tax Deferred Annuity	Insured Annuity	Variable Annuity
Inflation	4	1	3.5	1	3

Fees

It is difficult to rate these tools on a fee comparison because there are different structures at play. In the case of the prescribed annuity and the insured annuity, there is a one-time upfront fee embedded at the time you acquire the annuity and the life insurance. That is all built into the annuity purchase rate and the premium respectively. The corporate class funds will have an ongoing management fee, as will the variable annuity, but these too are different from each other, both in terms of the level of fees and the potential to tax deduct a portion of the fee. This was detailed previously in the description of each tool. The tax-deferred annuity has a combination of fees since it involves an annuity and a fund portfolio. The issue of fees and the impact they have on your assets and your income is examined in more detail in Chapter 4.

Tax Efficiency

Because I have used non-registered assets in all of the examples of the different tools and strategies, they are all extremely tax efficient.

MAKING YOUR BLUEPRINT WORK FOR YOU

1. The four considerations that every investor needs to weigh and balance are certainty, flexibility, probability and perpetuity. Different income delivery and investment vehicles will have strengths and drawbacks in all of these areas. That is why you don't necessarily put all of your assets into just one strategy. Employ them to best address what your priorities, objectives, preferences and tolerances are. You need to determine what is of most importance to you.

2. The three headwinds, which include taxation, fees and the ability to address inflation, are those things that will "drag" on the efficiency of any one investment option or income-delivery vehicle. So you need to be aware of how your choice or choices of tools is affected by these factors.

3. If you have non-registered investments in mutual funds or pools, they should be within a corporate class (also known as capital class) structure. There is no reason for them not to be. Be aware, however, that some of the major financial institutions do not offer this type of structure on their own "in-house" mutual funds. So you are not going to hear about "capital class funds" from advisors affiliated with these institutions.

4. Life annuities or term-certain annuities purchased with non-registered assets can receive prescribed tax treatment. The interest portion of the payment is deemed to be the same each year and this allows for some strategic tax planning. One of the strategies covered in this chapter was the Tax-Deferred Annuity, which combines the certainty of annuity payments with the tax-efficient growth potential of corporate class mutual funds.

5. Another guaranteed income strategy involves combining a life annuity with a life insurance. Insured annuities will deliver a high level of guaranteed income. The trade-off for the higher income is that there

is no access to capital because it is used to purchase the annuity income. The life insurance component replaces the capital, used to purchase the annuity, to the estate at the passing of the annuitant(s). Mortality credits may work to your benefit if you purchase a life annuity at age 75 or later. Purchasing a life annuity at a later age may help sustain a level of income even if your overall assets may have declined in value through your retirement. Purchasing a life annuity later in life is more common than you may think. For example, in 2009, one of the leading providers of life annuities in the United States reported that over half of their new annuity sales that year were to people age 80 and over.

6. Variable annuities are now offered by basically all of the major life insurance companies in Canada. They combine a level of guaranteed income for life with the potential for increases to that income if the underlying investment portfolio produces returns that exceed the payout and the management fees involved. There is flexibility to unwind the contract if necessary and that feature is a good one, as things will change throughout retirement. Traditional annuities will provide a higher initial income, but they lack the flexibility of the variable annuity. As is the case with all of the special tools and strategies covered in this chapter, it is strongly recommended that you not place all of your capital into only one of these vehicles.

11

INSURING YOUR BUILDING

The purpose of this book is to provide you with a step-by-step template that you and your advisor can use in putting together your retirement income blueprint. Although it is not the intent of this book to go into detail on health-risk management, it is necessary to make reference to this issue because of the potential impact on your retirement income and your income-producing assets. Assume that you have a $400,000 home and $400,000 in investments. In the morning mail, you receive the renewal for your fire insurance. The policy's premium is $1,500. You could turn to your spouse and say, "You know the premium is $1,500 and we've never had a fire in our home. In fact, there has never even been a fire in this neighbourhood. Let's not spend the $1,500 on insurance. If the house burns down, we'll just replace it by taking the $400,000 we have in our investment account and building a new one." That evening as you are watching TV, you see smoke coming out of the kitchen. I assure you that if this happened, you would run down to the insurance company with the $1,500 cheque in hand.

It's not logical or financially practical to put $400,000 at risk when $1,500 per year would cover that risk. Why is it any different with loss issues related to critical illness, long-term care or life insurance? As it pertains to health at age 65 and beyond, there is "smoke in the kitchen." This is the time that health-related risks are the greatest, and yet I find people not insuring those risks. Do not use your income-producing assets to self-insure at this time in your life. Investigate the use of insurance to transfer this risk.

Your personal health is your greatest asset. But it also represents one of the greatest risks to the health of your income and your income-producing assets. Most people mistakenly believe that the government will look after them as they become older and require care. And while governments do provide a level of care, the segment of the Canadian population over age 80 will double in the next 20 years and triple in the next 40 years according to Statistics Canada. This will put unbearable strain on an already overburdened, understaffed and under-equipped health care system. In Canada, the average cost, per year, for health care is just over $4,200 for those aged 65 to 74, just over $8,000 for those aged 74 to 84, and for those over age 85, it is approximately $16,000, according to the Canadian Institute for Health Information. That is a cost covered by the government, but through the taxes you pay. As the population ages and more strain is put on the health care system, governments may not be able to continue funding health care at these levels, putting more of the burden and more of the risk on the individual to provide for themselves.

Therefore, it is more important than ever to establish your objectives and priorities in the area of health-risk management and determine how this liability will be funded. There are some key issues here that need to be addressed. The more I work with retiring and retired clients, the more convinced I am about the importance of preparing for and managing health risks and the associated costs. There are several reasons for this.

- A person can lose his or her health either through a critical illness (defined later in this section) or by simply reaching a point where ongoing care is required. There are both emotional and financial costs associated with this for the individual afflicted, the spouse (who may very well be the primary caregiver) and the family.
- Shorter hospital stays mean longer at-home recovery and higher financial, physical and emotional costs. When you or your partner suffers a critical loss of health, the golden years turn to the olden years. That period of time between the last child leaving home and the first elder needing care is the time of greatest independence.

I have defined the prime retirement years in the same manner—
from the point when retirement commences until the first elder
needs care. This applies to either spouse in the case of a retired
couple. As a Boomer, you or your spouse may already be in the
role of caregiver to your parent(s).

- People needing long-term care are not going to go without it, but
  as the Boomers reach this point, the level, quantity and quality of
  care they receive will largely depend on their ability to pay for it.
- Disability insurance, or "income replacement," is a benefit few
  people would think of doing without while in their working years. If
  you are unable to work due to an accident or illness, that coverage
  replaces your earned income. When you retire, this coverage stops.
  You don't need disability insurance when you are retired. You no
  longer have an employment income that needs to be insured. But
  you should have "asset insurance" in the form of critical illness (CI)
  coverage and, ultimately, long-term care (LTC) coverage. After all, it
  is your retirement assets that are now providing income, and they
  need to be protected. Coping with the costs of a critical illness or
  long-term care could severely reduce or even deplete your retirement assets. This source of income should be protected.
- Even something as simple as dental health and prescription drugs
  can impact cash flow. Yes, these things do have to be looked after in
  retirement, and there is a cost associated with it. Within the last few
  years, major life insurance companies have made available health
  and dental insurance programs for individuals and couples. They are
  worth investigating as a tool to cover basic health expenses. There
  are various options and forms of coverage that can be acquired.

When it comes to funding potential health costs or care costs, you really
have one of two options. You can use your own assets or use insurance.
If you choose to use your own assets for health costs and want to leave
behind an inheritance, you may be more reluctant to spend those assets. If
health-cost issues and wealth-transfer issues are covered off by insurance,
you will have more discretion in terms of how you choose to use your
income-producing assets to fund your own retirement lifestyle objectives.

It is also necessary to include commentary on this issue because the use of insurance vehicles is going to involve the payment of a premium. And whether that is paid annually or monthly, it is going to represent an item in your cash flow needs.

As it relates to health costs, this is very much a risk-management issue. These costs could include a large lump-sum withdrawal for a procedure or travel for treatment. Or the costs could be smaller but ongoing and erode income-producing assets over time. It is an issue for the cash flow of the afflicted person and his or her spouse and could also negatively affect the income of the caregiver or survivor. You can't predict if and when these types of health-risk costs will occur. But you do need to address the possibility that they will occur.

Government Services

Provincial governments have programs relating to long-term care issues in place to assist people with some major health-related events. Long-term care (LTC) generally deals with providing non-acute nursing assistance to those who are restricted or prevented from being able to live independently due to an ongoing (or chronic) condition(s) or cognitive impairment. Long-term care may take place in the home or in a care facility. Long-term care is different from traditional care in that it is designed to maintain a level of independent living, not to provide a cure or improvement in the condition. The incidence of LTC needs is increasing for two main reasons. First, people are living longer. Advances in medical treatment and drug therapy have extended life expectancies. Second, hospital stays are now generally very short and the care that used to be delivered in the hospital must now be received in the home or in a care facility.

The range of long-term care services and facilities provided by government programs varies widely between provinces. Some of the restrictions for users include:

- qualifying for benefits by condition
- qualifying for benefits by income (means test)

- availability of services or facility
- limited choices and options
- limits on amount of assistance (maximums)

Ongoing care that is covered by government programs falls under two main categories—home care and facility care.

Home Care

The home has become today's recovery room. Shorter hospital stays, day-surgery procedures and limited hospital space all have contributed to this trend. Home care is a program of care delivered to a person in his or her home as recommended by a physician and provided by a licensed nurse or an authorized employee of a health-care agency. Any of the following conditions could qualify you for government benefits that will offset some of the costs of home care: an injury or sickness, the inability to perform two or more activities of daily living (ADLs), cognitive impairment or medical necessity caused by chronic illness. ADLs include eating, bathing, transferring (moving in and out of bed), dressing and toileting. The objective of most retirees facing the need for care is to remain in their own home for as long as possible. If care can be delivered in this setting, it will allow people the choice to maintain the additional degree of independence that being in their home affords them.

Home Care Costs (example)

In-Home Visits
$25 to $35 per hour (registered nurses or auxiliary nurses)
1 one-hour visit each day = $1,000 per month
$12 to $15 per hour (medical services aid)

24-Hour In-Home Nursing
$112,000 per year (licensed practical nurse)

Facility Care

The need for facility care can be triggered by the same impairments as described above under Home Care. But in these cases, more in-depth health- or personal-care services are required on a long-term basis. When patients enter a long-term care facility at the order of a physician, they may qualify for government benefits to offset the costs.

But in the case of facility care, in addition to qualifying for care by your condition, a financial, or means, test is applied to determine the level of funding for which you are responsible. Means testing for benefits is normally a function of taxable income from the previous year. This is the same means test that is applied to qualify for other government entitlements. There may also be an asset test that is used to determine the availability of or level of assistance. Most provinces in Canada have at least one means test to determine eligibility for benefits.

Facility Care Costs
Government facilities (fully funded)
Occupancy is 100 per cent
Waiting lists are in the 1,000s

Certified Facilities (government subsidized)
$1,600 to $2,200 per month (after subsidy)

Private Retirement Homes
$2,500 to $6,000 and more per month

What You Pay—the Per Diem

"Per diem" is Latin for "for each day." A per diem is basically the levy that is charged to you as the cost of being in a long-term care facility. It is an amount assessed over and above that which is already paid by government. The amounts are charged on an ability-to-pay basis and the measure to determine how much you are able to pay is based upon your net income from the previous year, less total tax payable. There is a different yet corresponding schedule that applies if the person receiving care is single or married. In the married context, the combined net income of the household is used, minus combined total tax payable. Each province has its own table of a per diem payable relative to net income, and there are different formulas for how funding or partial funding is provided. As your net income increases, in approximately $50 increments, the amount of per diem required increases. The following table provides a rough example using selected net income amounts.

TABLE 11.1: Manitoba Per Diem Rates, 2011

Net Income (Single)	Net Income (Married)	Per Diem		Per Month
< $14,785	<$45,024	$31.30	=	$939
$20,000	$50,000	$45.70	=	$1,371
$25,005	$55,280	$59.40	=	$1,782
$30,115+	$60,355+	$73.40	=	$2,202

Long-term care costs do qualify in the calculation of the medical tax credit if a licensed practitioner has referred the patient to a licensed facility. The credit can only serve to reduce taxable income, not net income. There are some ways to lower or avoid a per diem, including reducing your net income. This goes hand in hand with tax planning, which was discussed previously. Practically, your net income would have to be very low to avoid a per diem.

Even after an individual qualifies, it is essential to realize that each province sets limits on the benefits to be provided. Home care may be provided, but the number of hours and the number of visits may be limited. At the same time, there is no guarantee that existing programs and levels of government funding will stay as they currently are. The percentage of provincial budgets dedicated to health-care costs is continually rising and this will only accelerate with all of the Baby Boomers now entering their retirement years. Access to government-subsidized long-term care facilities is also regulated, and since this is the lowest cost alternative, long waiting lists exist in many provinces. The costs of these services, over and above any government assistance, will have to be paid by you.

What Are Your Options to Fund these Potential Costs?

Okay, I know what you are thinking on this topic, "That's all fine, but this is not going to happen to me." That is how we all think. But since the odds are nearly 50 per cent that it will, what plans do you have in place to address the care you will require and the costs associated with it? What I commonly hear, from those who really haven't thought it through, are the following courses of action (or courses of inaction to be precise).

My Spouse Will Be My Caregiver

That is a pretty common and simple answer. Keep in mind, however, that 41 per cent of those age 65 and over are single. In addition, 70 per cent of women age 65 and over are either single, widowed or divorced. And women tend to end up being the primary caregiver. As a man, I look at that as a trade-off for you being able to live longer than we do. So many times when I ask the question of who will be the caregiver, the man immediately jumps to answer. So here is a 225-pound guy with a spouse less than half that weight and she is supposed to be able to provide care for him. It sounds great as a solution, but it is not really going to work all that well if it needs to be put into action.

Seldom discussed is the impact, financially, emotionally and physically, on the person actually providing the care. In more than 50 per cent of the cases, the person providing care predeceases the person being cared for. What will life be like for the surviving person needing continuing care? There is still more to this issue than the monetary considerations of providing care. There is also a human cost in terms of the personal wear on the caregiver, the impact on his or her lifestyle and ultimate financial well-being. Who, in turn, looks after the caregiver should he or she eventually need care?

My Children Will Look After Me

Parents who want to have their children look after their care needs or children who offer to have parents live with them have absolutely no idea of the mental, physical, emotional, monetary and time demands to which they will potentially be subjected. At the same time, there is most often a level of care required that children, despite the best of intentions, are not qualified to provide.

Often, the care-giving duties fall upon the shoulders of one of the children in the family. This may be as a result of proximity, preference or even gender. Care may become an obligation that is unequally shared. This unequal and often overwhelming distribution of duties can be lessened to a great extent through planning and by implementing some tools to address costing issues. For example, children could purchase long-term care coverage on their parents in order to provide the proper care needed and at the same time alleviate their feelings of obligation. This could also serve to protect their inheritance.

Your parents likely had several siblings. But families today normally have 2, 1 or 0 children. That does not provide all that much opportunity to divide up the duties. And the other important issue is that most working families today require two incomes. Your children should not be expected to have to balance their work and the time required to provide your care. Have you chatted with the kids about this plan you have? Are they aware that this is what you are thinking? Do you really want your kids doing *all* of the things that have to be done to provide your care? Do they want to be doing those things? It is not that they don't care. I am sure that they do. But there is a huge difference between "caring" and "caring for."

The Government Will Look After Me

As detailed earlier in this chapter, the government does provide a level of care, but for you to rely solely on this is like relying only on your CPP and OAS to fund your retirement. You could do it, but what quality of retirement would you have? What choices would that really provide to you?

We are indeed fortunate that the government delivers "basic" services, with limits, in most provinces. Although this is a benefit, you still have to be aware that there are limitations that you will face, in the form of:

- quality of care
- standard of care
- consistency of care
- amount of care

With the aging population, the number of people moving into retirement and high government deficits that have ballooned in 2009 and 2010, there is going to be a limit as to what can be provided, which will affect the points mentioned above to an even further extent.

I Will Just Finance It Out of My Own Assets

Most people are not familiar with what their financial contribution will be toward the total cost. Do you know how the per diem system works in the province where you will be retiring?

The monthly payment (per diem) required from your household for facility care can change the cash flow dynamics substantially. It may have taken combined incomes to provide the retirement lifestyle being enjoyed. Now one income is basically being dedicated to what amounts to a second residence in the form of a care facility. How will that impact the non-afflicted spouse?

Transfer the Risk by Using Insurance

Transferring the cost risk through the use of insurance rather than your own retirement assets employs the concept of "discounted dollars." As you may recall, the concept of discounted dollars (paying pennies to get one dollar of benefit) is the fourth D of effective tax planning. The concept behind insurance is very simple. You and others like you make small contributions to a pool in exchange for protection from a particular disaster. This may be fire, auto coverage, life insurance or heath-risk coverage. Premiums for any of these forms of insurance are not deductible from income, but proceeds from a claim are not taxable when received. The term "discounted dollars" applies since what you pay in premiums is a mere fraction of the benefit you would receive from a claim.

I want to look at two insurance products that can help address these health-related costs: critical illness and long-term care. For each of these insurance vehicles I will provide a brief overview of what they are and what they do. You need to talk to your advisor about the details and the merits of either or both of these in your own situation.

Critical Illness (CI) Insurance

A critical illness is defined as the diagnosis of or the onset of heart attack, life-threatening cancer, stroke, coronary-artery bypass surgery, multiple sclerosis, Alzheimer's, Parkinson's, major organ transplant, kidney failure, paralysis, coma, blindness, deafness or loss of speech. Today in Canada, heart disease, life-threatening cancer, and stroke account for 80 per cent of the deaths, up from a total of 14 per cent in 1900. So your chances of being diagnosed with a critical illness are quite high.

At 40 years of age:
Out of 100 healthy males, 30 will have a critical illness by age 65
Out of 100 healthy females, 27 will have a critical illness by age 65

Between age 40 and 65, your chances of incurring or being diagnosed with a critical illness is 10 times greater than your chance of dying.

While the incidence of critical illnesses has increased dramatically, so has the survival rate. The costs incurred by the survivors of these illnesses can be substantial. Although the costs of basic treatment are currently covered through provincial health plans, the major costs of dealing with and surviving illness are borne by you and may include such things as:

- more immediate medical treatment
- the best physicians and facilities to treat your illness
- experimental or alternative treatments
- adapting your residence for special needs
- private care at home or a care facility "per diem"
- costs of extended travel or relocation
- costs of drugs and treatments not covered by provincial programs

The above expenses can have a seriously negative impact on your retirement assets and income. For example, the Canadian Cancer Society has estimated that two-thirds of the costs related to cancer treatment are indirect expenses not covered by provincial health-care plans. Without insurance to cover such expenses personally, your only choices may be to:

- use retirement assets (RRSPs, savings et cetera)
- sell fixed assets (house, cottage, valuables)
- settle for what treatment is available, when it is available
- impact other family members emotionally and financially
- reduce the retirement lifestyle of you and your spouse

CI insurance is not life insurance or disability coverage. It pays a lump-sum, tax-free benefit to you if you are diagnosed with a critical illness. The benefit is payable only after you have survived 31 days after incidence or diagnosis. If death should occur, your estate or beneficiary would be entitled to a refund of the premiums that had been paid.

There is also a refund-of-premium (ROP) option that repays to you, your survivors or your estate, at set points in time, the sum of annual premiums paid into the plan if no previous claim is made. Coverage can extend for as long as you live or for a defined period of time. The lump sum you receive can be spent at your discretion. While some people use it to seek treatment services outside of Canada, that is only one potential use for this insurance. Many times it is used for other purposes and expenses that have no connection with health care, including:

- clearing off debt
- allowing for a longer convalescence period before returning to work
- funding expenses for family to visit while you recover
- permitting you to return to work on a part-time basis
- allowing you to retire sooner
- allowing you to retire immediately

The greatest cause of illness is stress. All of the options listed above would be actions that would reduce stress. In addition, this coverage helps protect the retirement lifestyle of you and your spouse by protecting your income-producing assets. If you are retiring early and have left your health benefits with your employer, this becomes an even more important issue. You should at least cover off the time until the younger of either you or your spouse reaches age 65. The financial impact of a critical illness is magnified greatly if it occurs in your earlier retirement years.

Long-Term Care (LTC) Insurance

The main reason Canadians have a difficult time wrapping their heads around the concept of obtaining an external source of funding for their long-term care is that they believe that government and the current medical system will look after their needs. But they may be very mistaken in their assumptions. With the demographic realities of this nation combined with the extended longevity we will continue to experience, we will simply have more people requiring these services. At the risk of sounding callous, the facilities will be better and more readily available to those with the money to pay for them. For the rest of us, it will be a matter of accepting what is available, when it is available. Those who prepare ahead for this eventuality will have a more dignified and enjoyable experience at this point in their lives.

Acquiring LTC coverage does not mean being sent to a nursing home. What it does mean is that there will be money available to allow people to maintain their independence, freedom of choice, quality of life and dignity. In addition, you are protecting:

- your retirement assets
- your spouse's retirement/care
- your children's/grandchildren's inheritance
- your opportunity for charitable giving

Premiums are paid into an LTC plan for a limited period of time, even though coverage lasts for life. This premium period is determined by your age at the time the coverage is purchased. There are also policy options such as inflation protection and refund of premium riders. All benefits are received on a tax-free basis and are paid directly to the insured or their designated power of attorney (POA). There are no physical examinations to go through; you must only complete a basic questionnaire. Issue ages are from 40 to 80.

While critical illness benefits are purchased and paid as a lump-sum amount, LTC benefits are paid as a "daily benefit." There are different provisions for benefits payable for home care and for facility care. Various durations for benefits are another factor in setting up your coverage. Once again, either with CI or LTC insurance, there are so many options and variables that this is something that needs to be covered in depth with your advisor.

Ironically, as you examine these issues in more detail, your tendency may be to assume that these are issues you will never face, when, in fact, you would be the exception if you did not. For many reasons, CI and LTC issues should be addressed in advance. Proper planning can provide a course of action to follow and a mechanism for funding should this type of care be required.

The use of critical illness or long-term care insurance to fund these liabilities will ultimately provide you with more choices for care and/or treatment. The quality of life at that time will largely be determined by the ability to make choices. In turn, the ability to make choices will largely be determined by how much money is available for such purposes. The surge in the number of people retiring over the next 20 years plus the potential for greater longevity is going to put huge pressure on both government and private care facilities. Planning and the use of insurance can provide you with options for services that are going to increasingly be in demand.

Two Important Points to Remember about Insuring the Risk of Long-Term Care

First of all, the cost of not taking action is *not* zero. It is not the difference between paying nothing and paying a premium. It is the difference between paying a premium and paying for the cost of care . . . if you can afford it. You know the cost of doing nothing and you can calculate the cost of the premium. What you can't do is quantify the potential liability of the cost of providing care.

Second, and although the following statement is true at any time in your life, it is of particular importance when you are facing issues that deal with your health and living out your later years in comfort: quality of life is predicated on your ability to have choices. And often, money will be the prime determinant of whether or not you have choices. Empower yourself to be in a position to be able to choose.

Power of Attorney and Health-Care Directives

I don't want to get into estate planning, but I do want to touch on a couple of tools that may assist in protecting your income-producing assets from health-related costs and problems. The first is a power of attorney, signed while you are well, designating another person to look after your assets while you are alive. Such an attorney might do your banking, manage your investments and file your tax returns in the event that you are incapacitated, absent from the country or otherwise unable to attend to such matters yourself. Should you become incapacitated without having appointed an attorney, an Application to Court will be required, at considerable time and expense, to name a committee to look after your affairs. In some circumstances, the public trustee may take on that role. By signing a power of attorney now, you may avoid such complications.

Living Will (Health-Care Directive)

The second tool is known either as a "living will" or "health-care directive." This instrument gives advance written instructions on medical treatment you would or wouldn't want, should a time come when you become unable to make decisions or communicate. It also lets you name someone to make medical decisions on your behalf if you become incapable. This gives you peace of mind in knowing that your wishes will be carried out, even if you are unable to convey them. It also relieves others from the stress of having to guess what your wishes might be. You should be aware that there are certain differences in format between provinces. It is recommended that you review your living will on an annual basis. Having done so, you should initial and date it so that your doctor is confident that these are your current wishes. It would be appropriate for your doctor to have a copy of your directive in his or her file. For details on establishing a health-care directive, contact your doctor.

A Tax Note on Health Costs

There are tax credits available to those who are incurring medical expenses and who are providing in-home care for infirm or elderly relatives. One need not be retired or of a certain age to claim them.

The Medical Expense Credit

All *qualifying* medical expenses over 3 per cent of your net income will create a federal tax credit of 15 per cent. For example, consider a retiree with a $50,000 net income who has spent $1,900 on qualifying medical expenses

in the calendar year. Since 3 per cent of $50,000 is $1,500, only the remaining $400 qualifies for the medical expense credit. The federal credit is
calculated to be $60 (15 per cent of $400). Provincial credits are applied in
the same manner. A married or common-law couple can combine qualifying expenses and claim them on the return of one spouse. By claiming in
one name, the 3 per cent exclusion is applied only once. If applied to the
spouse with the lower taxable income, there is a larger balance of allowable medical expenses that qualifies for the credit. In the above example,
assuming $1,900 of expenses, if the lower-income spouse's net income was
$20,000, the 3 per cent limitation is calculated at $600, leaving $1,300 to
be applied to the credit—$900 more than if the higher-income earner had
made the claim. The resulting credit is a dollar-for-dollar reduction of tax
payable. There is a maximum for the 3 per cent exclusion. In 2011, it cannot exceed $2,052. This represents 3 per cent of a net income of $68,400.
The claim can be made for the best 12-month period ending in the tax year
(24-month period in the year of death). Hence, if the 3 per cent net income
limitation wipes out any tax benefits from the credit, it is wise to save the
medical expenses for use in the next year.

Some qualifying medical expenses include:

- payments to medical practitioners and nurses
- payments to dentists
- prescription drugs
- institutional care (nursing homes)
- hospital fees not covered by public health insurance
- costs of diagnostic procedures
- care and supervision of persons with severe and prolonged dis-
  abilities living in a group home
- costs of moving to accessible housing
- home and driveway alterations to accommodate someone with
  mobility impairment
- specific medical equipment and devices

A more detailed listing of the above, plus other eligible expenses, can be
found at the Canada Revenue Agency (CRA) website www.cra-arc.gc.ca.

The Caregiver Credit

A tax credit is available for caregivers who provide in-home care for infirm or elderly relatives. The infirm relative must be living in the same home as the caregiver. The credit is factored on the Caregiver Amount, which is $4,282 in 2011. If the infirm relative's income is in excess of $14,624, the credit is reduced. It will disappear entirely if income exceeds $18,906. These are 2011 numbers and will change since both the benefit and income brackets stated above will be indexed with increases to the CPI. If you are already claiming the amount for an eligible dependent (formerly known as equivalent-to-spouse), you can also claim either the infirm dependent tax credit or the caregiver credit. In other cases, claim either the infirm dependent tax credit or the caregiver credit, but not both. The net income level of the dependent will affect the amount of your claim.

MAKING YOUR BLUEPRINT WORK FOR YOU

1. Having a plan to cover health-related expenses prevents them from having a potentially disastrous impact on your personal assets and income and ensures the standard of living for both the individual affected and the caregiver.

2. Current economic conditions and demographic trends mean that government health-care options are going to be limited in the future.

3. Critical illness and long-term care insurance can provide for you and your family in the case of serious illness, meaning your income and assets can remain intact.

4. The forms of health insurance mentioned in this section are acquired with "health" and paid for with money. So the earlier this can be addressed and acquired, the better the opportunity to qualify for coverage and the lower the premium.

5. The premium for insurance will be part of your required cash flow and needs to be budgeted into your income needs.

6. Employ the use of health-care directives (living wills) and an enduring Power of Attorney. This will ensure that your wishes are carried out even if you are not able to communicate them at some point in the future. These documents also empower those who are looking after your affairs to act on your behalf without having to make life-and-death decisions that affect you.

PART
SIX

CONCLUDING THOUGHTS

12

MAKING THIS BOOK WORK FOR YOU

There you have it, an efficient Six-Step Plan to create retirement income. It has evolved since 1993 into the model that has been presented here. The planning and investment strategies that have been discussed here have also evolved. They have been tested over and over again, and they work—as long as people are prepared to stick with their blueprint.

There are a considerable number of moving parts to this whole process. The purpose of the blueprint, or Six-Step Plan, is to have all of these components moving in a complementary manner. So often, things are set up in such an ineffective way that parts of the process are actually in conflict with each other. And that leads to inefficiency and much unnecessary waste.

Each year, Baby Boomers are retiring in greater numbers. This demographic has had a dramatic impact on society in every phase of its existence, whether on music, politics, education et cetera. As a group of people who have always wanted to influence change and have control, they are now coming up to a time in their lives that is rife with change. And there many things in retirement that can't be controlled, only dealt with. Your retirement income will be built from the assets and entitlements that you have spent a lifetime accumulating. Creating your blueprint is essential in order for this to be done in the most efficient manner and in order to allow you to address and adapt to the many changes you will go through in your retirement years.

I have summarized certain key points under the heading Making Your Blueprint Work for You at the end of each chapter. In order to make this book really work for you, I would encourage you to go back and review those particular headings in the order they appear in the book.

I mentioned that in this book I would challenge some of the "old-school thinking" that still permeates much of the retirement income planning theory out there and that is still incorrectly being used as advice. You don't need a retirement income that is fully adjusted for inflation for 35 years. And in many cases, it is not beneficial to defer all of your registered accounts for as long as possible. And what about becoming more conservative with your investments as you get older? Perhaps this would be wise, but remember that you will still continue to need some element of growth in your accounts.

All the way through this book, I have talked about making things more efficient as you plan for and enter retirement. As part of this summary, I want to list the 10 most common inefficiencies:

1. Working with a financial planner but not having a financial plan
2. Working with an advisor who is not proficient in the area of income planning
3. Not consolidating your assets with one advisor
4. Not using the right mix of taxable and tax-advantaged income
5. Using personal assets instead of government pensions
6. Deferring income from RRSP accounts until age 71
7. Not using corporate class funds for non-registered accounts
8. Paying investment fees that are too high in exchange for what is provided
9. Making asset-use decisions with no thought toward the Income Continuum
10. Not considering the use of some form of health insurance to address that risk

You can compare these with your own situation, discuss them with an advisor and see what improvements could be made and what that would mean to you. You may be surprised to find out how many of these inefficiencies you have in your own situation.

Ticket to Ride

Here it is, blunt, front and centre. When you retire, your "ticket gets punched" and, Baby, you had better enjoy the ride. Because, as a friend of mine likes to say, "You are dead a long time." Why would you not seek to make the most out of this time in your life and the three "commodities" that you carry with you into retirement? Those three commodities are:

- your state of health
- your longevity
- your income-producing assets and benefits

It's funny that of those three, the only one that you can define at the moment you retire is your financial standing. And you can basically do that "right to the penny" (assuming it is still legal tender in Canada as you read this). The other two aspects are total wild cards. You don't know how long you will stay healthy or, for that matter, stay around! And with that in mind, allow me to conclude by drawing an analogy between your retirement and going on an all-inclusive vacation.

Assume you are going away for two weeks to an all-inclusive vacation spot. You've worked really hard and now you are ready for your reward. So to make this the "vacation of a lifetime," you turn to your spouse or partner and say, "Look, we really deserve this vacation. This time around, let's make sure we do some of those extra things we have always wanted to do on an all-inclusive vacation but that aren't part of the package—things like scuba diving, golfing, parasailing, excursions and the like." Your spouse agrees, and you are set to go on a vacation that you will never forget. But you pause, think it out in a bit more detail and suggest the following. "Let's just take the first week of our vacation and not do any of this extra stuff we want to do. Let's just get used to the climate, the sun, the surroundings and the facilities. Then we will do all of these neat things during the second week."

So, during the first week, you limit your activities and spend very little of your money, in anticipation of the second week. The first week is perfect. But, for the first three days of the second week, the weather turns quite bad. Well, at least you still have the last four days. But then you or your spouse become sick for the last four days. The second week is a write-off and you didn't get to do any of the really special things that you had planned in order to make this the vacation of a lifetime.

You sit down when you come back home, think through what has happened and here is what you say: "Next time we go on a vacation, we are going to plan it out in a much better manner. We are going to prioritize those special things that we want to do and we are going to plan them into the vacation, doing the most important things first and the less important things later in our trip. That way, if we unexpectedly have an illness or bad weather, we would at least have had the opportunity to do a few of the things that are most important to us." And the point of my story is this: You can always go back and redo your vacation. You can't go back and redo your retirement. This type of planning is what the blueprint can help you think through, put together and execute.

So plan your retirement as I have just described. Set your priorities and make it happen. Don't just let it happen. In that way you can live it to the fullest. I stated at the very outset of this book that the purpose I had in writing it was to help you make the best use of your money and your time in retirement. It is my hope to have you merge the two of these together to make this fabulous time in your life that much more fulfilling. I have had the privilege of watching people do just that, and it is both a rewarding and inspiring thing to witness. Get it planned out, get your blueprint put together and enjoy your retirement! Remember, you need to take action. You need to investigate your options if you are using an advisor, and you should expect to derive the most out of your retirement by merging your time with your money. How long a life you live will be determined by fate. How fulfilling a life you live will be determined by you.

APPENDIX

Life Income Fund (LIF) Comparison by Province

The following chart compares features of provincial and federal LIFs, including spousal consent requirements, earliest LIF purchase age and payment age, allowable reasons for unlocking funds, death benefit information and marriage breakdown information.

	BC	AB	SK[6]
Supplier must be on approved carrier list	Yes	Yes	No
Spousal waiver/consent required to purchase	Yes Form 3 - Spouse's Consent to Transfer Locked-in Pension Funds to a LIF	Yes Pension Partner waiver on Transfer to a LIF, DC RIA or Annuity	N/A[6]
Earliest purchase age	54	50	N/A[6]
Earliest payment age	55[1]	50	N/A[6]
Earliest annuity payment age (purchased with LIF funds)	55[1]	50	55[1]
Full year maximum income in year of transfer from LIRA or pension	Yes	No. Maximum income prorated based on number of months in the LIF for the year.	No longer available for monies from a LIRA/ pension plan[6]
Unlocking due to Shortened Life Expectancy	Yes	Yes	Yes
Unlocking due to Financial Hardship	No	Yes	No
Unlocking due to Small Amounts	Yes	Yes	Yes
Unlocking due to Non-residency	Yes	Yes	No
Other unlocking provisions	No	No	No
Death benefit entitlement to spouse	Yes, unless waived	Yes	Yes
Death benefit locked-in	Yes, to spouse	No	No
Spousal portion locked-in on marriage breakdown	Yes	Yes	Yes
Owner required to purchase annuity at age 80	Not required	Not required[7]	Before Jan. 31 of next year
Unisex (post) rates on annuity purchase	Yes	Not required	Yes[6]
Maximum payment calculation	Greater of CANSIM factor[4] and earnings	Greater of CANSIM factor and earnings[7]	CANSIM factor

1 Or earliest age at which funds would have been annuitized under pension plan

4 For Quebec, Manitoba, Nova Scotia, and British Columbia, the CANSIM rate is adjusted to determine a reference rate. This reference rate may be higher than the CANSIM rate used by other provinces and may result in a different maximum payment. The BC maximum calculation is the greater of this applied CANSIM rate factor and the income earned in the previous year of the LIF.

6 Effective April 1, 2002 Saskatchewan pension legislation no longer provides for the sale of a LIF if the monies are coming from a pension plan or a LIRA. **Only transfers from existing LIFs are acceptable**. Other than a life annuity, a Saskatchewan prescribed RRIF (PRIF) is now the only other possible retirement income option for a Saskatchewan LIRA or pension plan. Any LIFs currently held must now be administered contractually (based on regulations that were in effect at March 31, 2002).

7 Effective August 10, 2006, Alberta removed the requirement to annuitize at age 80 and changed the LIF maximum calculation to the greater of the applied CANSIM rate, the investment earned in the previous year in a LIF and the RRIF minimum.

	MB	ON (Old)	ON (New)
Supplier must be on approved carrier list	Yes	No list exists	No list exists
Spousal waiver/consent required to purchase	Yes Pension Waiver (Joint and Survivor 66 per cent)	N/A	Yes Consent forms part of Application
Earliest purchase age	Anytime	N/A	54
Earliest payment age	Anytime	N/A	55[1]
Earliest annuity payment age (purchased with LIF funds)	Anytime	N/A	55[1]
Full year maximum income in year of transfer from LIRA or pension	Yes	N/A	No. Maximum income prorated based on number of months in the LIF for the year.
Unlocking due to Shortened Life Expectancy	Yes	Yes	Yes
Unlocking due to Financial Hardship	No	Yes	Yes
Unlocking due to Small Amounts	Yes	Yes	Yes
Unlocking due to Non-residency	No	Yes	Yes
Other unlocking provisions	Yes	No	Yes 25% within 60 days of transfer
Death benefit entitlement to spouse	Yes	Yes, unless waived	Yes, unless waived
Death benefit locked-in	No	No	No
Spousal portion locked-in on marriage breakdown	Yes	Yes	Yes
Owner required to purchase annuity at age 80	Not required	Not required	Not required
Unisex (post) rates on annuity purchase	Yes	Yes[3]	Yes[3]
Maximum payment calculation	CANSIM factor[4]	CANSIM factor	Greater of CANSIM factor and earnings[9]

1 Or earliest age at which funds would have been annuitized under pension plan
3 For post-reform benefits where a pre/post split is provided at the time of purchase, Manulife will split sex-distinct and unisex funds into two separate policies
4 For Quebec, Manitoba, Nova Scotia, and British Columbia, the CANSIM rate is adjusted to determine a reference rate. This reference rate may be higher than the CANSIM rate used by other provinces and may result in a different maximum payment. The BC maximum calculation is the greater of this applied CANSIM rate factor and the income earned in the previous year of the LIF.
9 Effective July 1, 2008, ON "New LIFs" are available for monies transferred from an ON LIRA, Old LIF, or LRIF.

	PQ	NB	NS
Supplier must be on approved carrier list	Yes	Yes	Yes
Spousal waiver/consent required to purchase	No	No	Yes Consent forms part of Application
Earliest purchase age	Anytime	Anytime	54
Earliest payment age	Anytime	Anytime	55[1]
Earliest annuity payment age (purchased with LIF funds)	Anytime	Anytime	55[1]
Full year maximum income in year of transfer from LIRA or pension	Yes. Must complete Quebec Declaration Schedule 0.9 and 0.9.1	Yes	Yes
Unlocking due to Shortened Life Expectancy	No (LIRA only)	Yes	Yes
Unlocking due to Financial Hardship	No	No	No
Unlocking due to Small Amounts	Yes	No - LIRA only	Yes
Unlocking due to Non-residency	Yes	Yes	No
Other unlocking provisions	Yes: Additional temporary income	Yes: One-time partial LIF unlocking	Yes: Additional temporary income
Death benefit entitlement to spouse	Yes	Yes	Yes
Death benefit locked-in	No	No	No
Spousal portion locked-in on marriage breakdown	Yes	Yes	Yes
Owner required to purchase annuity at age 80	Not required	No	Not required
Unisex (post) rates on annuity purchase	Not required	Yes[3]	Yes[3]
Maximum payment calculation	CANSIM factor[4]	CANSIM factor	CANSIM factor[4]

1 Or earliest age at which funds would have been annuitized under pension plan

3 For post-reform benefits where a pre/post split is provided at the time of purchase, Manulife will split sex-distinct and unisex funds into two separate policies

4 For Quebec, Manitoba, Nova Scotia, and British Columbia, the CANSIM rate is adjusted to determine a reference rate. This reference rate may be higher than the CANSIM rate used by other provinces and may result in a different maximum payment. The BC maximum calculation is the greater of this applied CANSIM rate factor and the income earned in the previous year of the LIF.

	NF	PBSA
Supplier must be on approved carrier list	Yes	No list exists
Spousal waiver/consent required to purchase	Yes Consent forms part of Application	No
Earliest purchase age	54	Anytime
Earliest payment age	55[1]	Anytime
Earliest annuity payment age (purchased with LIF funds)	55[1]	Anytime
Full year maximum income in year of transfer from LIRA or pension	No. Maximum income prorated based on number of months in the LIF for the year.	No. Maximum income prorated based on number of months in the LIF for the year.
Unlocking due to Shortened Life Expectancy	Yes	Yes
Unlocking due to Financial Hardship	No	No
Unlocking due to Small Amounts	Yes	No
Unlocking due to Non-residency	No	Yes
Other unlocking provisions	Yes: Additional temporary income	No
Death benefit entitlement to spouse	Yes, unless waived	Yes[2]
Death benefit locked-in	No	Yes, to spouse
Spousal portion locked-in on marriage breakdown	Yes	Yes
Owner required to purchase annuity at age 80	Before Dec. 31 of that year	See below[8]
Unisex (post) rates on annuity purchase	Yes	Yes
Maximum payment calculation	CANSIM factor	CANSIM factor[5]

1 Or earliest age at which funds would have been annuitized under pension plan
2 Spouse may redirect death benefit entitlement to a dependent of the deceased owner, as defined under Section 8500(1) of the Income Tax Act
5 Federal PBSA uses the actual CANSIM rate, whereas the provincial pension jurisdictions default to a minimum 6% CANSIM rate. This means that the maximum payment for PBSA LIF contracts will be lower than those administered under other pension jurisdictions when the CANSIM rate is less than 6%.
8 Effective September 21. 2006, Federal pension legislation removed the requirement to annuitize at age 80, however, this does not automatically apply to contracts in existence at that date. Existing contracts must be renegotiated between the client and the financial institution administering the LIF in order to remove this requirement.

ACKNOWLEDGEMENTS

The John Wiley & Sons editorial team, Retirement Income Industry Association (RIIA), Walterharder.com, RBC Financial, Standard Life, Dynamic Mutual Funds, Desjardins Financial, and The Knowledgebureau. Thank you for your shared passion in this project.

INDEX

ABOUT THE AUTHOR

Daryl Diamond is a recognized leader in the financial services industry. His practice, Diamond Retirement Planning Ltd., focuses on advising pre-retirement and retirement clients on the income structures, investment strategies, and estate conservation issues that are unique to those groups. He is active in educating advisors and their clients on retirement planning. He runs seminar programs and has designed training programs for three large Canadian financial institutions—Standard Life, Dynamic Mutual Funds, and the Royal Bank—to educate advisors on retirement income planning.